BLACK BEAR

MY LIFE STORY

MERRILL OSMOND

Copyright © 2025 Merrill Osmond.

All rights reserved.

No part of this publication may be reproduced, stored in a retrieval system, or transmitted in any form or by any means—electronic, mechanical, photocopying, recording, or otherwise—without the prior written permission of the copyright owner, except for brief quotations used in reviews or critical articles.

This is a work of non-fiction. The events are portrayed to the best of the author's memory. Some names and identifying details may have been changed to protect privacy.

A CIP catalogue record for this book is available from the British Library.

ISBN: 978-1-918077-18-6

First published in 2025 by Quartz Press.

quartzpress.com

This book is dedicated to my sweet family, Mary and my children, Travis, Justin, Shane, Heather, Troy, and Sheila.

IN OTHERS' WORDS

※

'The Osmonds were who we were because of Merrill. He defined our sound. He was the lead singer, and I was considered back up to him even though I went on and had my own career. But Merrill, he had the rock and roll voice, the sound, the range so it was really him that gave us our sound and the ability to hit big in the 70s.

As a brother, he's the best!'

— DONNY OSMOND

'Besides being one of the most talented singers in the family, it is Merrill's ability to feel compassion, tenderness and love for others that truly stands out to me. I'm sure that made him a great performer, lyricist, and songwriter.

He has always been there for me, and, for that, I am eternally grateful.'

— MARIE OSMOND

'Though Merrill and I were four years apart, as brothers, we worked closely together in sharing many of the same gifts and talents. We loved music and writing many songs together, painting with oils on velveteen, photography, and creating productions for both television, movies and live events in celebrating our love of God, Family, Freedom and Country.

Merrill invited me to join his production team, Osmond Entertainment, that he and Tommy Walker, the manager of Disneyland, had created, which produced the Opening Ceremonies for Ronald Reagan's Presidential inauguration and also for George W Bush.

At a young age, with Merrill's middle name being D, for our mother's maiden name of Davis, our parents would often call Merrill by the nickname 'Mellow D.'

That is very appropriate as one of Merrill's musical strengths is the creating of awesome melodies for many of the songs that we wrote together.

Merrill was also called the 'peacemaker' of the family, and if a family member or a fan was ever found being left out or with their feelings hurt, Merrill would often pull them aside and give a listening ear and some comforting counsel with them.

Merrill fell in love and married Mary Carlson from Heber, Utah at a young age, the love of his life. Merrill and Mary had six children together that also had musical talents, especially Troy, who was the most talented in playing the organ, even the Tabernacle Choir Organ at Temple Square in Salt Lake City.

The hardest thing Merrill and Mary had to face in life was the early passing of Troy. But with faith and understanding of God's 'Plan of Happiness' they knew that Troy would once again be reunited with their family when we all return back to our heavenly home again.

Merrill remembers many detailed events of his life as he recorded them in his journals. So I am sure he will be sharing some in this book that will bring memories of so many great moments of his life with you from his travels around the world.

Merrill, I believe in you, your leadership and creative genius, along with the love you always have for all others. We spent so many years entertaining and working together, not only as brothers but also as best of friends. Eternity won't be long enough as we continue to work together 'side-by-side' into the future.'

— ALAN OSMOND

'Merrill has a very commercial, awesome voice that made him our lead singer. He was also a great bass player and entertainer. He always had so many creative ideas for shows, new businesses, and other ventures. He was a good leader and was respected among us all.

I loved writing songs with my brother. Both he and Alan were my buddies. We would spend all the spare time we had working on new and different types of songs.

Merrill is a very charismatic person who attracts everyone. He related well with our managers and others in showbusiness, so everyone felt comfortable and relaxed. He was very much a people person and went out of his way to be very friendly to everyone, especially the fans and they all still love him.

Growing up with Merrill, I always enjoyed hanging out together. He would give anyone the shirt off his back. He and I always wanted to be doctors. We talked about naming our office Dr Osmond and Osmond. I was always really impressed with the compassion and empathy he showed Virl and Tom. He was very considerate and loving and he especially loved our parents.

I'll love you forever, brother Merrill, and cherish all the good times!'

(written just a month before his passing on January 1, 2025)

— WAYNE OSMOND

'It is an honor to say something about my brother Merrill. We've worked side by side for so many years, building projects that mattered, not just to us, but hopefully something much greater than us. We are ten years apart, almost to the day, but that never stood between us. We worked together as one.

Merrill was our lead singer, though he never sought that title. He never had that desire. He didn't crave the spotlight, what he did crave was purpose, something meaningful to God, to our family and to those we served through our music.

If you want to understand the heart of the man we call Bear, listen to him sing "He Aint Heavy, He's my Brother." That's where you'll find—not just his voice, but his spirit.'

— JIMMY OSMOND

'Merrill has written so many wonderful songs for the world and is a great producer of many things.

I will always love you, Merrill Osmond.'

— DOLLY PARTON

'Merrill Osmond is an icon and a great example for all of us.'

— GARTH BROOKS

'I have known Merrill for over 42 years. He is an icon in the entertainment industry. Starting as the lead singer and music writer in The Osmonds, Merrill quickly became known around the world for his smooth, silky voice and animated personality. He had tremendous success as a television producer for many productions, including the Donny & Marie Show. Even with enormous success in the entertainment industry, Merrill's greatest attribute is his humility, kindness, and love for all people, especially his fans.'

— RICHARD L. HILL
ATTORNEY AND FRIEND TO THE OSMOND FAMILY

'We often remember people for what they did. For Merrill Osmond, that might mean the music—the amazing voice, the harmonies, the sold-out concerts, the song writing, the years at the top of the charts. But the real story of Merrill's life is not what he has done, but who he is.

There are voices that do more than sing—they heal, uplift and remind us of something greater. Merrill Osmond is that voice.

He is not only incredibly musically gifted—he is spiritually sensitive and a visionary. This is the side of Merrill Osmond many don't see. Whether comforting a stranger, standing up for the forgotten or simply offering a smile that makes you feel seen, Merrill embodies a rare grace and a presence to everyone he meets.

Merrill has been able to bless *millions* throughout his life. Not just through the songs he sang or his incredible voice, but through the quiet ways he listens. Through the compassion he shows, even while carrying pain of his own and it often made his struggles more intense.

He once said the greatest disease isn't physical—it's the feeling that you're not enough. But he also came to understand this: we are enough—not because of what we do, but because of who we are.

I have had a wonderful teacher over the years in Merrill and I feel blessed to have worked with him and his family for so many years now. I have witnessed miracles occur through him and seen so many lives touched by his compassion to others in all walks of life as he recognized those who need it the most.

This book will enlighten you as to what Merrill Osmond is truly all about.'

TRACEY BEAUMONT
**PERSONAL ASSISTANT TO MERRILL OSMOND,
2009—PRESENT**

CONTENTS

IN OTHERS' WORDS i
FOREWORD 1
BEFORE WE BEGIN 3

CHAPTERS

ONE – Now and then 5
TWO – 'You're not a very smart young man, are you?' 13
THREE – Shining examples 23
FOUR – 'You are the peacemaker of the family' 31
FIVE – Fame and fortune 45
SIX – Mary, my darlin' 57
SEVEN – Starstruck 67
EIGHT – Rewritten history 73
NINE – Close shaves and testing times 79
TEN – Rubbing shoulders with important people 93
ELEVEN – Squandering money is wrong 109
TWELVE – Heroes and a saint 117

THIRTEEN – Black Bear 127

FOURTEEN – Celebrity survival 147

FIFTEEN – Troy Dean, The Jelly Bean 161

SIXTEEN – Glittering galas for good causes 167

SEVENTEEN – Serenity.. 177

EIGHTEEN – When the show couldn't go on 183

NINETEEN – A life's mission 189

TWENTY – It's hard to say goodbye 193

TWENTY ONE – A man like me 199

MOTHER AND FATHER

BY OLIVE OSMOND.. 209
SOME OF MOTHER'S MEMORIES 219
SOME OF FATHER'S MEMORIES.. 223

TRIBUTES

THE BAND 233
TRIBUTES TO MY CHILDREN 237
FOOTNOTE 241

FOREWORD

by
RON CLARK
Former publicist and spokesperson, Osmond Entertainment

Merrill Osmond stands today as one of the truly great entertainers of our time.

Ever true to his musical birthright, he has captivated audiences the world over with his unique voice and performance style spanning nearly 68-years as lead singer of The Osmond Brothers and on the many family albums and concerts he has helped produce.

Records totalling over 100 million in sales have proven his singular arrangements, sound, unique voice and delivery style which has earned him a personal fanbase that has withstood the test of time.

This book is Merrill's story. It represents his legacy, and it presents the reader with the opportunity of receiving a rare and transparent look inside the daily lifestyle of a world class entertainer and very private family man.

The integrity found in each chapter is such that reading his words and personal feelings will leave the reader with a sense of belonging to this kind soul as a friend and confidant. His relationship between performer and follower is uniquely wonderful in today's entertainment world.

I invite you to read and enjoy all of which he writes—friend to friend—as he addresses fame and fortune, and then an unexpected downturn creating sobering moments and new directions. This biography is told in his warm, sensitive, gentle manner—a voice for all who face happiness and defeat.

The pages ahead open a door of transparency rarely exposed in such a raw and personal manner. He speaks of his growing up in the unrelenting world of showbusiness with siblings who became his best and only friends. He opens the front door and presents a behind-the-scenes look at a husband, father, grandfather, and faithful follower of a Christian lifestyle that he embraces willingly and openly.

For nearly five decades I have had the privilege and opportunity to travel with and represent the Osmond name. During this period, my friendship and knowledge of Merrill has been unwavering, honest, and sincere. He is a man of integrity, discernment, and unassuming nature. In my opinion, he stands indeed as one of the truly great people and entertainers of our time—a superstar who still shines on and off stage.

From the moment he first stepped on stage as a child star and member of the internationally renowned Osmond Brothers Quartet, to the printing of this long-awaited new book, he has recorded stories of a life well lived through success and seasoned with deep and scarring challenges. He writes of his lifetime over six decades spent before audiences throughout the world—giving, giving, and then giving some more. Herein he writes with a warmth and candor that opens long-closed doors of achievement and failure. In all accounts, however, he has risen to the top again and again to self-improve, taking the hard knocks on the chin.

BEFORE WE BEGIN

I want to make it clear that this memoir is more than just a retelling of events—it's a testament. A testament to the power of music, and how it has shaped my life, expanded my vision, and taught me what it can truly accomplish when it reaches the heart of someone willing to listen.

This memoir is also an effort to set the record straight. Over the years, there have been many misconceptions, misunderstandings, and outright rumors surrounding the Osmond family. These have caused confusion, pain, and at times, a distortion of truth. It's time to clarify some of those things with honesty, dignity, and respect.

Throughout my life, I have faced many struggles—some public, most private. Many of these challenges I've kept to myself for deeply personal reasons. But I've come to believe that being open about them might serve a purpose. If you've ever struggled quietly, as I have, then maybe in these pages, you'll find not just a story—but some comfort in knowing you're not alone.

You'll find that as you read this, there were many who came into our lives with good intentions—but also those who deceived us, who defrauded us, who embezzled from us and caused incredible division. The kind of division that could have torn our family apart.

But I want to be clear: I will not be using these pages to tear anyone down and certainly not any member of my family, but what happened, happened. And while the truth deserves to be told, it will be told with compassion and grace.

Because trauma has a way of exposing what lies beneath. When the dark clouds roll in—when everything you've built seems to teeter on the edge—that's when a person discovers who they really are. That's when strength rises. That's when courage is forged.

And that's when a legacy is either broken… or built.

Ours was built.

I hope you enjoy the book. Writing it has been a fascinating journey for me—one filled with reflection, learning, and healing.

— Merrill Osmond

Chapter One

NOW AND THEN

On a cold, wet Wednesday night in Blackburn, England, I found myself on stage singing many of the hit records my brothers and I had performed over the years. Just before the final song, I glanced behind me at my band and singers and everything seemed to stand still.

In that quiet moment, all I could think about was how incredibly blessed I have been to share the stage with some of the greatest musicians. It felt like a dream, a gentle haze.

Then suddenly, the crowd erupted as the band launched into the opening chords of 'Crazy Horses.' That amazing feeling didn't fade, it grew. I watched as the audience sang, danced and moved with the rhythm. They knew every word—and they made sure I knew they knew every word too.

The energy in the air was overwhelming. As I stood there, something inside me just paused. I looked out at the crowd singing, smiling, completely alive in the music and it hit me how rare these moments are. I felt this wave of gratitude, like I was standing in the middle of something much bigger than myself. It was a deep sense of love and connection. In that moment I realized how blessed I have been to be part of something that brings people together like this.

The venue was King George's Hall. Most of those attending that night were mature ladies. Over the years, having written many of the songs like 'Crazy Horses,' 'Hold Her Tight,' 'Back on the Road Again,' and other heavier rock songs, I had always hoped that we would have been able to attract more guys to come to the shows.

My seventieth birthday was coming up, and I was still working hard instead of sailing off into the sunset with my wife and children. My entertainment career really started at the age of four. That's a long time to have worked. There are some who would say, 'Oh, performing isn't work, it's just an opportunity to have some fun.' I'm not saying that music and the opportunity to sing were negative experiences; in fact, it's just the opposite. But the number of rehearsals, time spent away from family and friends, and trying to perfect our trade daily did take its toll on us throughout the years.

I was performing in the Windsor Suite, where the standing capacity was 750. The next night, it was a similar scene in Milton Keynes, followed by Enfield, London on the Saturday and Butlins Holiday Resort in Skegness on the Sunday playing to 3,000 fans. As a member of The Church of Jesus Christ of Latter-day Saints, I've always struggled because of my deep faith to perform any show on a Sunday. It is the Sabbath day and a day of rest. But in some cases, where a promoter insists on that day, there's not a whole lot you can do about it.

It seemed like a world away from the Osmonds' heyday when, in my late teens and early 20s, my brothers and I would perform in vast, high-profile stadiums, all packed with tens of thousands of screaming teenage girls. Wembley Arena, Madison Square Garden, you name it, we played it.

Who can forget that terrible moment in October 1973, when hysterical fans caused a viewing balcony to collapse at Heathrow Airport? It injured 18 girls and got us banned for a long time from

CHAPTER ONE

flying back into Heathrow airport for any future concert tours. We had to fly into Scotland and travel by a secret train down to London.

Well, that was then, and this is now, and I was more than happy to be in Blackburn in October 2022 with all those amazing, loyal fans who still wanted to watch me perform live.

To this day, I still can't wrap my head around the fact that anyone really wanted to come and see me. Coming to see Donny, Marie, or Jimmy was one thing, but I was just the lead singer of The Osmond Brothers. I have never felt special by any means, but I will always be humble and grateful for the chance to sing the songs that bring happiness to all the people who attended our shows.

I was once told by someone very close to me when I was young that I would never make it in showbusiness on my own; that I needed to stay as one of the group and never step out. And in fact, that one statement has literally crippled my ability to see anything special in whatever I did on my own.

Months earlier, in April 2022, I had performed my last shows in the somewhat glitzier setting of Las Vegas. This was at The Westgate, which used to be The Hilton, where Elvis had his residency all those years ago. My band Pat, Phil and Dave had flown in from England just for these shows, with my dancers and singers, Abbie and Louisa, and soundmen Ralph Walsh and Matt Boyles. I called them all my 'Dream Team.' The Westgate had provided the best stage crew and everyone was excited for the shows.

That one last emotional concert was more than just a performance, it was a profound moment for me in more ways than I can explain. I don't speak about this often but when the spirit whispers that it's time to step away, you listen. I have followed that voice many times throughout my life and it's helped guide me through some of my hardest trials.

Unless there's a very special cause, my days on stage have come to a close. There may be the odd event I attend or produce, but as far as all the touring is concerned, this really was 'goodbye'. It's not out of regret, it's out of peace. A peace that comes from knowing when it's time.

Despite the negativity that constantly raged in my mind about my inability to stand alone, I was still managing to have a lot of fun! That time was the best therapy I could have ever asked for after spending a lifetime on the edge.

Of course, I still get nervous before singing a song or speaking to any group that wants to hear me talk about my years in the entertainment industry. It may sound strange, but I am far more at ease performing to thousands of people than giving a talk to a hundred or so.

Even if I could, I wouldn't want to turn the clock back and return to the way things were in the 70s. I wouldn't want to deal with all the relentless stress, anguish, and depression that I experienced back then.

The old need for perfection hasn't gone anywhere; it still hovers within my mind as I feel that I owe it to whatever audience comes to see me to deliver my best performance. Heck, I even get nervous when asked to give a two-and-a-half-minute talk in church! Can you believe that? I'll critique the heck out of myself when I sit down and think about what I just said.

Not many of you know this, but the relief I felt at not having to keep one eye on the audience and one on my brother Alan's right hand, coiled like a spring for any sudden twitch of his first finger, followed by a raise—that was the subtle sign for me to switch chord and up the tempo no matter if we were mid song or about to close one.

All of us are perfectionists and what Alan was doing was just keeping us in pitch. Back then, we were literally trained to try and

CHAPTER ONE

stop anyone who would get up in the audience to either go to the bathroom or exit. If we felt we were losing our audience, Alan, being the leader, would stop the song immediately and yell out a whole different song to hopefully divert that person from leaving. As I look back, that took the word 'pacing' to a new level. We obviously had a fast repertoire up our sleeves in case this happened.

We had a system, if someone was off, the brother standing next to him would quietly press a thumb into his back: Up if he needed to raise the pitch, down if he was too sharp; no words, no drama, just a subtle signal that said *'you're blowing it, fix it!!'*

The ones I really felt bad for were the members of our band at that time, especially those who had not memorized our repertoire. Switching in the middle of a song, playing it in a different key, and keeping smiling all along took a very good individual, but boy, did we always have a good band!

I can remember a time when a 20,000-seat arena was full of not just hysterical fans, but a group of people that were going through mania and started to attack the stage. Pass-out lines (fainting girls) began to form, and everybody was brought up on stage. We laid out smelling salts, and anything the police could do to try and wake them up was not happening. The other problem was that because of the commotion, security ordered us off stage.

When things died down a bit, we went back on stage and started up again. Ten to fifteen seconds later, the attacks began again. We were ordered off stage as the pass-out lines began to pile up in greater numbers. All I can say is that throughout the two-hour concert, we only played one song: Crazy Horses. After the show was over, we looked out into the arena, and every wooden chair that was on the floor was broken. I mean hundreds and hundreds of chairs.

We found out that a few days before we even started performing in that venue, some gals had snuck in and navigated themselves into a small space between the stage and the scaffolding that held it. Our security was baffled, how, in the middle of our show, they would appear from out of nowhere and attack us on stage.

There were other stressful situations that I was finally able to deal with when I worked with the guys. I literally had to starve myself all week just to squeeze into one of those Elvis-inspired white jumpsuits that became such a part of our image. Throughout our years on stage, with a wider waist than each one of my brothers, who seemed to always naturally be skinnier than me, trauma set in, and I became scared of food in general.

To be completely honest, if I did eat something that would cause any weight gain, I would throw it all up before going on stage.

Today, I can just be a white-haired grandpa of 15 wonderful grandchildren. I can wear whatever I want on stage and have a bass strap slung across my shoulder that doesn't need to match the color of the jumpsuit.

Now, singing alone, that doesn't matter anymore. The last few years of my life have truly been years of therapy for me.

I cannot even begin to tell you how relaxed I have been on stage in more recent times. I don't even need to attend soundchecks anymore as the band have everything ready in place. They know me well enough to run through the show together before I even arrive. I've never been able to do that.

Even if I must switch on to autopilot and rely on my subconscious rather than my memory to get me through, I'll do it. Throughout the years performing alone, what made me happy was to stare into the faces of those who were either singing the songs along with me or in a state of wonderment, listening or reliving the song they probably fell in love with years and years ago.

Judging from the expressions on their faces these days, they still seem to enjoy themselves, which means I can continually relax more.

CHAPTER ONE

There are truly no words to describe what comes over me when I can see and feel the connection from those who have paid hard-earned money to come and see me. Even today, I still am humbled by this. It is such an overwhelming feeling that I experience when I see and feel the connection from those who have paid to see me. The song 'Let Me In' is particularly special to me because everyone sings it with me. It is probably the song I love the most. Indeed, there are times when I become so emotionally overcome that I have to stop and let the fans sing it to me.

We have felt so welcomed in all the countries around the world that have graciously opened their hearts to welcome us into their living rooms, either through all the TV shows we did or all the thousands of records that we recorded throughout the years.

In every country we visited over the years, the one country that seemed to become our second home was England. I was always told that if the English love you, you're accepted for life; but if they don't like you, leave quickly. I guess we did okay in having them like us because we spent more than half of our career in England and the rest of the UK.

It's been well documented that the reason we even started singing was to help raise money to buy hearing aids for our two older deaf brothers, Virl and Tom.

As a very sensitive personality, entertaining would have probably been the last thing I would have wanted to pursue, but destiny seemed to point its finger at us. Today, I can honestly say that I have wholeheartedly accepted every problem, every moment of stress, everything that caused hope to depart, and every mistake that I made. Had it not happened, I wouldn't be the person I am today, and you know what? I sort of like this guy now!

Writing my weekly message on Facebook has become a kind of therapy for me. I've quietly struggled with many infirmities over the years, and having a platform to share those thoughts has brought healing—not just for myself, but I hope for others who may be facing similar trials. If even one person feels a little less alone because of something I've shared, then it's worth every word.

Through a tremendous amount of therapy and the discovery that I had no serotonin in my brain, my healing began to kick in. These Friday Messages have sparked a huge, welcome response and I will continue to post these, knowing they are helping many people.

Ultimately what has truly got me through has been having a relationship with my Lord and Savior, Jesus Christ. Where I was weak, He strengthened. When I became lost, He found me. When I suffered from anxiety and depression, He soothed my soul and gave me a miraculous understanding of His eternal love for me. And when I made mistakes, He forgave me and continues to forgive me as I still fail at times.

Chapter Two

'YOU'RE NOT A VERY SMART YOUNG MAN, ARE YOU?'

As a youngster growing up in Ogden, Utah, my dream was to be either a pilot, a photographer, or a doctor. It surely was not to be an entertainer. I really did envision myself flying my own jet as a doctor!

I would wear a stethoscope around my neck, examining my family as they walked through the hallways at home. I had a little doctor's black bag full of M&M sweets and a set of plastic fake shots that I'd poke into their arms. Looking back, it was sort of funny because everyone seemed to catch on to my little passion and would come to see me if they had a cold or were sneezing. It was great fun. I had my initials, M.D.O., put on a door in a little corner room my parents prepared for me. The MD made me truly feel like I was the genuine doctor in the house. But when I got into my teens, it became pretty clear that my destiny would lie somewhere else.

Showbusiness and education were not a good mix back then. Our school lessons were usually squeezed in when we weren't performing. At a very young age, being backstage, in TV studios, and living in hotel rooms became the norm. As I look back at those interesting times, I always said I could be comfortable just living in a trailer house.

We had correspondence courses and private tutors who traveled with us as we went off on tours or remained with us at the TV studios to help with our studies during breaks in our rehearsal schedules. Being on the road and practicing our routines daily became normal to us. In many ways, we lived like the Von Trapp family in 'The Sound of Music.'

Yet our education was always a priority, especially for my mother. She came from a family of teachers. My grandfather Davis was a principal at a high school in Ogden, Utah, and bless his heart, he would do everything he could to ensure we learned the basics of math, reading, and history.

My grandfather and I were very close, and he knew I was getting very little sleep trying to keep up with our intense schedule. He often helped me with my tests but made me promise to review what he had done for me to ensure I understood. The correspondence course I took came from the American School out of Chicago. I looked through my journals the other day and saw my report cards—I got straight As and even A plus on every test score throughout the years.

In those early days, my parents built a little schoolroom in our attic where we had our own desks, chalkboards, and whatever else my mother needed to help teach us our schoolwork. Because my two oldest brothers, Virl and Tom, were deaf, Mother also had various computer-like devices to help them understand speech concepts. Certain colors would light up when the pronunciation of specific words was said correctly. My mother spent hours daily working with my two brothers.

My parents even arranged for experts to come over to help us with special science experiments. We had people come in to teach us about painting and photography.

CHAPTER TWO

I had only made it to the fourth grade in public school. After that, it was simply correspondence courses and private tutors overseen by my mother that allowed us to acquire a basic knowledge of the ABCs. So, my formal education was not as good as I had hoped it would be as I look back at my life. But on the other hand, being street-smart was truly an education that very few people ever had. For that alone, I am grateful. However, if the entertainment side of my life had ever ended, trying to find a basic job would have been extremely difficult for me. Thankfully I married my sweetheart, Mary, who is so well-educated, and she provided our children with an incredible education and a solid foundation.

Music and all the musical instruments you could imagine were always around our home. We were not very wealthy back then, so if someone in the family wanted to play, let's say, a banjo, they would take a lesson and then come back home to teach the rest of the family what they had learned. My mother, being a wonderful saxophone player who had played in big bands for years, was very influential in having us all play the saxophone.

I still remember the day when the company called 'Fender,' who build guitars and basses, negotiated a deal with my father to supply us with those instruments in return for advertisements on the various shows we did. After one of our rehearsals, all this equipment was set up in our home rehearsal hall. When all the brothers saw the instruments, everyone gravitated to the one they liked. Brothers Alan and Wayne especially went for the guitars, leaving the bass for whoever was last in to pick out their instrument. So, that day, I became the bass player of the group!

There was also a drum set from a company called 'Ludwig.' Jay immediately got on those drums and became an amazing drummer over the years. The four of us became the band initially. Donny would join later and he took the piano very seriously, becoming extremely proficient at that instrument. One thing I regret is not having learned to play the piano. It could have opened tremendous opportunities to understand chord structures better. But understanding how the bass fit into the chords allowed me to hear the rest of the harmonics.

When I was alone without Alan and Wayne to help fill out the chord structures, I would take a little cassette recorder, use my bass to establish the chord I heard in my ear, and compose songs. I would then get with my brothers and sing the melody and the basic chord for them to add the additional harmonics to complete the song. The blessings that were given to us to hear all of this came from learning and practicing barbershop harmony over the years.

Our parents always kept instruments like trumpets, saxophones, clarinets, flutes, banjos, guitars, xylophones, and even bagpipes around to challenge us to create even more musical experiments for our writing. It was all about learning whatever we felt could enhance our musical abilities.

I credit my mother for constantly being there for each of us and encouraging us to never give up on our passions. All that early training became extremely helpful when we were challenged every week to do something different on The Andy Williams Show. In any case, had we not learned a variety of instruments, the chances of us being on The Andy Williams Show on a weekly basis would never have come about.

But not all that happened was good in my youth. There was a man named Ron Myers, who was hired by our parents to tutor us in our formal education. This guy was extremely smart and willing to take on the challenges we, as a family, had to face in our basic formal education. One day he decided to challenge each of us with the American College Testing program (ACT), the standardized test used for college admissions in the United States. It was established in 1959 and could only be taken by anyone over 13 years old. I don't

CHAPTER TWO

remember how old I was when I took it, but I must have been younger than 15 because it was around that age when Ron's influence over our family's education abruptly ended.

Ron told me I needed to take an IQ test. I did the test, and I remember him looking at me and laughing and saying, 'You're not a very smart young man, are you?' He never gave me my score, but his harsh words caused damage to my already low self-esteem. Those words have remained with me to this day. I am recalling this incident now because I found it again in my journals. Ron Myers was a very cruel individual who seemed to take pleasure in making people feel stupid and bad about themselves, especially me.

Ron's reign of terror finally ended when we lived in Arleta, California. It's embarrassing for me to even write about this, but one day after a night full of rehearsals, we were so exhausted that we just dropped into our bunk beds. There was a fairly large guesthouse attached to our home. Because of the long hours, rather than going into the house to sleep, we would just jump into our bunk beds and try to get a few hours of rest.

Ron happened to be sleeping in one of those bunk beds directly under mine. Knowing our religious beliefs, he knew that any carnal thoughts or actions contrary to our upbringing would be rejected. Around three o'clock in the morning, as my journal describes, this 40-year-old man, thinking that I was asleep, climbed up to my bed and started to touch me. I was terrified—trapped in silence. The moment burned into me, leaving a trauma that would follow me for years. What made it worse was that Ron knew our values—our strong moral boundaries. He crossed a huge red line, violating not only my trust but everything our family stood for.

Confused and scared, I didn't know what to do, so I just kept pretending I was asleep and prayed and prayed fervently for him to stop. I tossed and turned, trying to avoid what he was doing to me.

Then, out of nowhere, our family dog, Fuji, started barking at the door. That sudden sound startled Ron. He jumped off in a panic. That moment gave me just enough time to escape. I jumped up and ran to the house to tell my parents.

I raced into my parents' room, woke them up, and told them what had just happened. My father jumped out of bed, ran over to the guesthouse, grabbed Ron by his pajama collar, and pushed him against the wall. I had never seen my father so mad and upset. At that point, my peaceful, loving, angelic mother stepped in and said, 'George, don't do that. There are other ways to handle this.'

My father stood there for a few seconds, trying to decide what to do next. Then he finally let go of Ron's collar and, in no uncertain terms, told him, 'You have five minutes to get off our property, and don't you ever come back here again.'

Ron did as he was ordered, and that was the last time I ever saw him. Today, I imagine, this would be dealt with very differently to how it was in the 60s.

Because of that one incident, the trauma still haunts me. Victims of abuse carry invisible scars—ones that are painfully difficult to erase. I have great sympathy for others who have endured similar pain, because I know how deep it goes.

All I do know is that abuse has sadly stuck with me long after Ron Myers went to his grave.

My lack of a formal education and my natural nervous disposition, combined with anxiety which was caused by my training in the perfection of barbershop harmony, made me fearful of making mistakes and failing at anything I was asked to do. It was all about perfection. Even to this day, I feel inadequate when I meet people with incredible knowledge and doctorate degrees learned through hard work.

In 2017, I broke down in tears when I was contacted and presented with an honorary doctorate degree in humanities at Dixie

CHAPTER TWO

State University in St. George, Utah. I was so honored at the grand old age of 64 to finally be able to say that I am now a doctor! It was a special day; Donny came and sat with my family as they watched me proudly when I was presented with the degree.

When it came to ego or pride, it was crushed very early in my life. The examples set by my parents kept me grounded and established the foundation of humility front and center. With nine of us children all learning the same trade, it took a lot of discipline and hard work to keep us in line and learn to be grateful for every blessing. We were brought up to believe that anyone who succeeded in any vocation was to be applauded, not envied.

There was a moment when I was nine years old, performing live on The Andy Williams Show, that caused me a great amount of stress and massive anxiety. Even today, when I perform, I recall that very moment when a huge mistake was made.

The four brothers were sitting on the steps with Andy Williams, and each brother was given one line to say. That one line was on cue cards in case I had a hard time remembering what to say. I rehearsed that line over and over for three days so I wouldn't make a blunder.

Well, I blew it big time. The line was simply, 'When he first put his pants on, he tucked his tails into his pants like a shirt.' When the little red light on the camera came on, I literally froze. I looked at the cue cards, but my mind was so scrambled that even that didn't help.

I mumbled, 'When he first put his tails on, he tucked his pants into his shirt like a shoe.' Everyone just stared at me. I remember feeling the color drain from my face, unable to take back the sentence I'd just uttered. No one in the audience laughed; they just stared at me.

Andy Williams stopped for a second and said, 'Oh, do you mean when he first put his pants on, he tucked his tails into his pants like a shirt?' I said, 'Oh yeah, that's it.' Then the audience roared with laughter. Literally millions of people watching this on TV did something to my mind that even today causes me to shudder when I'm given any line to say.

As I became more popular with the brothers, so did my problems. I was very young and naïve, a little country boy dealing with extreme anxiety and huge expectations. I remember performing in Sweden during what they called the Midsummer Night Festival. Nearly 200,000 people turned out, and we were the headline act among five other performers.

There were so many people that I couldn't even see where the crowd ended. My mind was working overtime trying to remember the words in Swedish. We had a song released in that country that almost everyone in the crowd knew. Well, do you think I could remember the words? Nope. I froze in my shoes while the other brothers sang the song.

There was another show we did in Sweden where there was a segment in our performance in which we would all play saxophone solos. One at a time, we would walk on stage and play our solo part. We would then run towards the curtain while another brother would come out with his saxophone and play his solo part.

Well, here I go again—I ran off stage at the wrong time while brother Jay came running on. He hit my head with his saxophone and blood started pouring out all over my white suit. But that old expression that everyone knows: 'The show must go on,' was ever present. As the song concluded, all the brothers came out to finish it. Blood was everywhere. The crowd started yelling for me to quit, but no, I stayed there and finished the song with the guys. Brother Alan stepped up to the microphone and said, 'This song should've been called Blood, Sweat, and Tears.' Then people started to laugh—thank goodness!

There were times throughout my young age that even though we were sick and shouldn't have gone on stage, we did it anyway,

CHAPTER TWO

and with smiles on our faces. I remember one time, I felt sick and throughout the show, I remember running off and throwing up in a bucket, then running back on to finish the song. There were seriously no other options. The show did go on.

I was always shy and frightened as a young boy. And I remember being bullied at times in school. I was known as Bucky. This was the name everyone used because my front teeth always stuck out. I finally got braces to correct the problem, but that name has been used by all my siblings throughout the years. I was walking home one day from school when I noticed a guy starting to follow me. The faster I walked, the faster he walked. I finally dropped my books and started running as fast as I could. I glanced back, and lo and behold, that kid was running faster towards me. I thought I was going to die. Was he going to beat me up? If so, why? I finally made it to the front of our house.

I looked back, and that kid was no more than 20 feet from me, just standing still and staring me down. He looked like the devil ready to pounce on me. I quickly ran inside and told my father about it. He said that if it ever happened again, he would go to the school and complain to the principal. I really tried to get out of going to school the next morning, but my parents insisted that I go. I was again so scared as I made my way to school. Luckily, he wasn't following me. But after school, there he was again, standing alone outside by a tree waiting for me. I was so scared that I wet my pants.

I obviously had to get home somehow. I ran so fast that my heart was beating literally out of control. And once again he was running right behind me, picking up speed and almost caught me. But I did get to the house, quickly opened the door, and ran inside, crying my eyes out. I told the story again to my father. He ran outside to try and find this kid, but he was already gone. My father started wondering if I was just seeing things and making it up. The following morning, after not sleeping much for a whole week, I got up to do my morning chores.

My father drove me to school and went with me into the principal's office to tell him about this bully. The principal got up and told me to come with him to show him who this guy was. We went from classroom to classroom. Finally, I saw him and pointed him out to both the principal and my father.

The principal warned him to never bully me again, or he would be expelled. I thought for sure that would stop him, but it didn't. The principal then asked a couple of physically large guys to walk with me back home, which really did help. But eventually, the police had to get involved. I don't know whatever happened to this guy, but being so shy, that experience is another that has never left me. The two guys who helped me finally made me realize that assistance can be there if I just asked for it.

I wasn't the only one being bullied during that time. There was an incident where my brother Wayne started to walk home from his school. I think he was in sixth grade. We had been told by the producers of The Andy Williams Show that if any of us got sick or hurt, we would not be able to appear until we got better. So that ended sports and anything else that could possibly get our bones broken or give us black eyes.

Walking home from school one day, Wayne was harassed by two guys. He came to a stoplight and had to wait for the light to turn green before he could walk to the other side of the street. I've no idea where they got it from, but these two guys took a large hat pin and rammed it into his behind.

Retaliation was not an option; any kind of fight was just not allowed. Gritting his teeth, Wayne accepted his fate and when the bullies had left him alone, he cried the rest of the way home. His behind may have been sore, and his pride dented, but he was free of a black eye which would have kept us all away from the camera until it healed. We had to be grateful for small mercies.

Chapter Three

SHINING EXAMPLES

❧

As far as role models for love, marriage, and family life in general were concerned, I didn't need to look any further than my own parents.

They were an amazing couple. The world watched them raise us. They literally became second parents to many fans around the world who were looking for advice. People could trust them; they had integrity, and they proved to be true believers in the gospel of Jesus Christ. They were true saints. Fans would refer to them as Mother and Father Osmond.

Many remember that our mother ran the Osmond fan club for so many years. She and my brother Virl created a magazine called Osmonds' World. My mother wanted to let every fan know how much she truly loved them. She kept a detailed journal that talked about all the people she tried to help along the way who were struggling. She had one of the biggest hearts I've ever known. Osmonds' World became hugely popular literally throughout the world, and even today I have fans asking me to sign their copies of the magazine they have collected and saved all these years.

One of the sweet journal entries I read one day was about my father. She said, 'I like him more every day. I saw him, and I thought nobody could look as handsome as he did. Not long afterward, we went on our first real date. I remember almost every detail of that evening.'

My mother loved big band music. She belonged to a small dance band in high school and played her E-flat saxophone, which was her constant companion since the seventh grade. But even though she loved to play music, she loved to dance even more. When she found out at one of the supper dance events that my father was going to be there, in her own words, she said, 'I'm sold on him.'

My father confided in my mother how he had dreamt of having a home of his own, but that he had known a lot of unhappiness as a child. Now he was having some health problems as a result. Not wanting to be a burden to anyone, he thought it was best for him to remain single.

But my mother couldn't see it that way and loved him enough to take care of him. Knowing he had been visiting his doctor, she made an appointment to see the doctor herself and ask just how serious my father's condition was. She found out that he had severe nerve issues.

When my father told my mother that he thought all he really required was some good home cooking and tender, loving care, that was all she needed to know. Mother quietly created a little campaign to change his attitudes. She began by letting him know how much he meant to her. And really, that was all my father needed. In fact, she wrote that he was flattered by the attention.

A few months later, he had the misfortune to fall from a moving train and he badly sprained his ankle. As soon as he recovered, he told my mother that he was going to California to relax on the beach and think things over.

About a week later, my mother received an intriguing letter from him, which she kept for years in an old scrapbook. It read along the lines of: 'I've been lying here on the beach thinking about life in

CHAPTER THREE

general. I'm 27 years old and should have settled down long before now. I'm glad I didn't, though, or I wouldn't have met you. I am glad I found you. If you think you love me enough, let's make some serious plans.' He enclosed a small silver ankle chain which she wore for many years.

In her excitement, our mother made the mistake of confiding in some of her friends at work. One girl who also liked him began spreading gossip. Almost instantly regretting her decision, our mother worried that it would upset our father, and she was right. When he came home from California, he had heard the talk, and it made him distant and quiet.

Heartbroken, she eventually decided that if my father didn't think enough of her to get things out in the open and discuss them properly, maybe she should forget about him and start dating other men.

'But I just couldn't,' she wrote. 'I couldn't bear the thought of losing him. I wasn't happy in anyone else's company.' Her anguish ended when her friend Velva cunningly set her up with a blind dinner date. Our father was in on the plot as he was the surprise date.

After a candlelight dinner at Velva's house, they danced to the music on the radio. When they stopped by the fireplace, my father told her he had bought a little present and challenged her to find it. Behind a picture, she found a small box containing a little diamond engagement ring. My mother spoke about laughing and crying with happiness; she felt her prayers had been answered, and the two of them began making wedding plans.

In sharp contrast to my father's early years, my mother herself had enjoyed a wonderful childhood. She was born in her grandparents' cabin in rural southern Idaho on May 4, 1925. Tom and Vera Davis were both well-educated with big hearts. My grandfather taught in a small local schoolhouse. It was from him that my mother inherited her lifelong love of books and learning.

Vera, a soft, brown-eyed, sweet lady, loved playing the piano at all the town dances. The year before my mother was born, she had lost her own mother during the birth of her 11th child.

My grandparents had a rich pioneer Latter-day Saint lineage. Grandma's maternal ancestors had heard about the Latter-day Saint missionaries on the streets of Durham, England, in the 1860s. They sold everything they possessed to board a ship for America to continue their religious beliefs.

When they arrived in New Jersey, they answered the call of the Mormon Prophet, Brigham Young, to go to Coalville, Utah, and be part of a mining expedition to gather the much-needed coal during that time frame.

My mother's maternal grandparents, Benjamin Thomas Nichols and Olive Laverna Booth, were extraordinary people. They were constantly called upon to help heal people in the mining towns where they lived. Instead of calling a local doctor, people called Benjamin and Olive. They kept a stock of pharmaceutical products on the top shelf of their pantry, including consecrated oil, camphorated oil, mustard, clean cloths for mustard plasters, and clean white sheets to make beds for the sick.

Benjamin was a very faithful and religious man who strongly believed in the power of prayer. When he laid his hands on the heads of the sick and anointed them with consecrated oil, he and his patients believed they could be healed by the power of God. Benjamin had a very humble heart and dedicated his life to the Lord Jesus Christ. During the flu pandemic of 1918, Benjamin and Olive spent much of their time at the bedside of their neighbors. Although the pandemic killed many millions of people worldwide, they were fortunate to escape it themselves. It always comforts me to think that maybe this is where I get my own desire to help people.

CHAPTER THREE

My mother was also close to her paternal grandparents, Samuel W. Davis and Maryanne Martin, whose parents had followed a very similar path to Benjamin and Olive.

It probably won't surprise you to know that with a surname like Davis, they originated from Wales. Landing in Pittsburgh, they worked in the coal mines, which enabled them to earn the money to travel across the country, settling with the body of Latter-day Saints in Utah. Sometime later, after he was widowed, Samuel built up a homestead in the small town of Samaria, near the Utah-Idaho border. They too had a rich ancestral history of strength, hard work, and commitment to family and faith.

My mother's earliest memory was waking up on a big bed in a cabin house and discovering that she was all alone. Sliding off the bed backwards, she ran through the house, searching for her mother. She went to the back door and called for her mom who was across the field, picking wild currants to make Jell-O. The relief and joy that my mother felt when her mother answered her call reassured her that she would be back with her soon. That memory never left her.

It's significant to me that her first memory was about being lost and returned safely to her mother's loving arms. My mother believed that the fear of being lost or abandoned is a common one, and that home and family are such an integral part of our sense of security and identity.

The fact that her mother lost her own mother less than a year before giving birth to our mother may also have explained the extraordinary passion with which she cared for me and my siblings. Coming from a good and strong loving family background had naturally given my mother the security, self-confidence, and optimism that my father's past didn't allow him the luxury of having.

As loving and supportive as my mother's parents were, they thought that at 19 she was way too young to marry our father and discouraged the union. My mother turned to Heavenly Father, praying that it would all work out.

It did, and on December 1, 1944, the two of them were married for time and all eternity in the Salt Lake City Temple. My mother describes in her journal that it was a beautiful, solemn, and sacred ceremony. Following a reception at her parents' home, they began their married life together. Our father built a tiny little home. It consisted of one room with dividers, but my mother found it a cute little place.

Despite all of her positivity, my mother was truly an introvert by nature, and she needed my father just as he needed her too. Because my father suffered from a lot of negative issues due to his nerves, he became very depressed easily. But our mother was right there by his side to help calm him and try to take the negative thoughts and feelings away, assuring him that everything was well. Doing that made her feel important and needed.

Throughout my life and the lives of my siblings, whenever we had a problem and were troubled, our mother would do exactly what she did with our father. She would comfort us by saying, 'This too shall pass.' This is a saying my siblings and I have used many times in life.

My father was a very frugal man. He believed if you take care of the dimes, the dollars will take care of themselves, whereas my mother loved to spend, and her theory was, 'Work like mad, but occasionally enjoy the fruits of your labors. You're entitled to have nice things if you earn them.' This achieved a good balance between the two of them.

They were both very diligent in saving their money. My mother was a secretary, and my father became a cabinet maker after leaving the railroad. When they were expecting their first child, my brother

CHAPTER THREE

Virl, they were able to buy a two-acre plot of ground and felt they had enough money to start building a home.

In my mother's journal, she talks about having problems with her pregnancy that made her extremely ill and miserable to continue working. My father's health and nerves had given him problems from working too hard as well.

Because of my father's constant determination to be the breadwinner, he quit what he was doing to find something other than 'pounding nails,' as he called it.

They settled into their new home, and my father got a job selling advertising for a local radio station. Our mother reassured him that she would help him in any way that she could by keeping records, making appointments, and filing away documents that he needed.

My father gave it all he had. And because of that, he won the confidence of several local businessmen, and soon his commission check was growing a little larger each month. His self-esteem began to get stronger. He flourished in that business and made a comfortable living for the two of them.

At that point, though, they could've never guessed in their wildest dreams what the future held. Some days when my father was working out of town, my mother would pack a lunch for them. She would take her books and handiwork and go with him.

One of her pet projects was embroidering a white christening gown, which was intended to become a family heirloom. The design that was etched on it was a family tree. Each child blessed in it was to have their initials embroidered in one of seven set spaces.

Little did they ever imagine that they would be adding two more spaces to those seven for the nine children that they would bring into this world. Nor did they know that their family would become known around the world as The Osmonds.

Chapter Four

'YOU ARE THE PEACEMAKER OF THE FAMILY'

~~~

If you want a true insight into the Osmond family, I suggest the best place to start would be at an Osmond family party or reunion. These events have taken place throughout the years and are quite rare now, but the memories of these moments will always be cherished. There will obviously be different takes or various remembrances that each sibling would recall, but here's mine.

There was one particular reunion that I'll never forget because it was such a professional event. We were all together and it was like a well-produced convention—everything well-paced and very organized. Because of the training we all went through at a young age, whether it be a television production, recording our music, a stadium spectacular, or even producing the opening inaugural ceremonies for President Reagan, we all became perfectionists.

Any lag of time during the reunion was scrutinized by all of us, and we would make suggestions to whoever was in charge of the reunion to tighten things up. At one event, Alan even created a firework display in the back of the field to close the get-together.

As a family, we were close to each other. We always made special attempts to help each other in whatever project individual siblings were overseeing. The events surrounding our Friday night get-togethers, which we called our family home evening, were always unique because our parents asked each of us to be in charge each week in turn. There would be singing, sharing stories to read, and we even had a boxing ring set up to see who could knock each other out first.

Our mother would go out of her way to prepare a meal that day, often asking each sibling to come up with their own menu ideas. I remember asking her to prepare the Merrill Osmond salad, which was macaroni and shrimp. Each sibling had their own special favorites. Even though the dishes didn't match most of the time, it was just a pleasant moment for all of us to get together, share a meal, and talk to each other.

Our father, who was working round the clock trying to provide for his family, always felt a little guilty because he wasn't around as often as he wanted to be. He was running a real estate company, an insurance company, a post office, plus serving in the bishopric of our church ward almost daily.

Our church, The Church of Jesus Christ of Latter-day Saints, always encouraged members to take one day a week to gather the family together. I'd say that this was one of the keys that helped each of us stay united and appreciate the foundation for family unity. Usually on a Saturday night, it was a tradition to have everyone load up into the family truck or rambler car to go see a movie at an outdoor theater.

This interaction with each other kept the bond strengthened to hold tight to our values and assist each other in our various endeavors.

CHAPTER FOUR

Making sure this happened every week led to future events that none of us could have ever imagined. It was all about good and solid parenting—discipline combined with unconditional love for one another. When a problem arose, it became all our problems. Our family councils on a weekly basis dealt with everything and anything that caused negative issues.

I'll never forget the day when our parents decided to take all of us on a trip to Yellowstone National Park. We would not only camp out at times but also go fishing together in those beautiful streams and lakes. On this one trip, our father began singing a favorite childhood song of his called 'The Old Oaken Bucket.' I remember Alan starting a harmony part to our father's lead. How the rest of us were able to hear additional harmony parts was quite unique as by the end of the trip, going home, we were literally singing barbershop harmony together.

Father would often suggest that we sing at church functions, community events, and even local fairs. It wasn't pressure, it was actually a lot of fun. Calls began to come in, asking us to perform at larger events. The bigger events paid us around $60—probably just enough to cover the gas it took to get there.

Our grandfather Davis loved what we were doing so much that he wanted to film us singing some songs and send them out to people who might want to hire us. On one trip, our parents decided to take us down to Los Angeles to hopefully get an audition with Lawrence Welk. We met the Lennon Sisters, who tried to get us an audition, but Lawrence Welk never had the time for us to sing for him.

Because of our disappointment, our father announced, 'Let's all go to Disneyland and pick up our spirits.' Our mother always dressed us alike, which bugged me throughout the years, especially when we were trying to find our own personal clothing because all our clothes looked exactly the same for each of us. However, it turned out to be fortuitous. We finally got to Disneyland, bought tickets to go in, and right there on Main Street, a bicycle built for four with barbershop singers came into that area.

Like us, barbershop singers always dressed alike. When they saw us, the Dapper Dans—which we soon learned was their name—stopped and asked if we were barbershop singers. We said yes, and they then, right on that street, asked us to sing a song. We did, and they sang a song to us. We went back and forth, singing our songs while a crowd began to gather around us.

The entertainment director of Disneyland, named Tommy Walker, was watching all of this unfold. At the end of our fun experience with the Dapper Dans, Tommy Walker came up to us and asked if we wanted to meet someone very special. We, of course, said yes.

Taking us into one of the rooms off Main Street, we discovered that sitting right there was Walt Disney himself! Tommy Walker told Walt he needed to hear us sing. I'll never forget that moment. Each one of us froze in our shoes. We were shocked that we were meeting the man himself. Walt said, 'Sing me a song.' I don't recall where we got the derby hats and moustaches from that we wore, but we sang a song to him called, 'I Want a Girl Just Like the Girl That Married Dear Old Dad.'

Having been trained to do everything perfectly, we set into motion to perform that song. Well, brother Jay kept losing his mustache, and his hat would fall off. Walt began to laugh. Each of us was so embarrassed that this was going on that it became extremely stressful. Our father, in particular, was so upset that he stared right at Jay with a bit of anger.

Our father had a stare that was frightening. The song came to an end, and Walt Disney began to applaud and continued to laugh. We apologized for the mistake, and he surprised us by saying, 'Are you kidding me? Keep it in the act! It's perfect!'

CHAPTER FOUR

Right then and there, he wanted to hire us to walk the streets of Disneyland, singing songs just like the Dapper Dans did. We were obviously shocked. But we did walk the streets of Disneyland for a long period of time.

Tommy Walker was producing a TV special called 'Disneyland After Dark' and asked if we would be on that show. We prepared for a 15-minute presentation, and after the performance was over, the show was edited and sent across the country on a network TV channel.

Andy Williams' father, Jay Williams, happened to see the show and we reminded him of his boys, the Williams brothers, who performed the same way that we did. So he reached out to our father and asked if we would come back down to California and audition for his son, Andy Williams. We came into the network studio and into a rehearsal hall where Andy's production team was sitting. The late, great Andy Williams no less said, 'My father tells me that you're a pretty good little barbershop group. Sing us a song.'

I remember singing two songs back-to-back, and the group applauded. Then Andy asked, 'Sing one more.' The song 'Take Me Back to Baby Land' was next. Then and there, Andy asked us to be on one of his weekly shows and I remember just being so happy. To make a long story short, we did perform that one song sitting on the steps with Andy Williams in what he called his 'Informal spot.' We thought that would be all he would offer.

Well, I guess the response mail that came in must have been enormous. People wanted to have us perform again on his show. And indeed Andy did ask us to do another show, but there was never a contract, so unless we proved ourselves by doing something new and different every week, we were not invited back. This turn of events caused us to literally change our lives.

We learned to tap dance, we learned to ice skate, we learned to play Dixieland music, we learned how to play piano. We played rock 'n' roll songs, we learned how to juggle, and even how to ride unicycles. You name it, and we did it. We did everything possible to create something unique every week. He kept us on his show for about seven years.

Those TV shows gave us a worldwide audience. We would travel to countries like Sweden, learn to sing in Swedish, and had hit records there. England was a good market for us; even Japan saw us on that show and asked us to come there. We literally were going somewhat around the globe singing our songs together. Andy Williams told us that our singing on his informal part of the show became one of the highlights, generating millions of letters from impressed viewers who wanted to keep us on his show.

Having tremendous anxiety and self-esteem issues so young, not to mention moments of depression, created a tremendous amount of stress on me as a person. We were known as the 'One Take Osmonds' because of the hours we would work in our guest room behind the house. We would learn our songs and new routines with absolute perfection. While others on Andy's show might not have their routines down, ours was always perfect. A mistake was just not allowed.

Brother Donny and our sister Marie showed up at this time and began to also start performing on The Andy Williams show. Even our little brother Jimmy, at a very young age, was one of the big hits of Andy's show. During those days, with only four network channels, it wasn't just a few million people watching us but nearly 50 to 60 million people were tuning in.

We eventually moved into the 70s, where our careers became extremely overwhelming. The song 'One Bad Apple,' our first number one hit, started a recording career that would last 65-years plus for some of us.

The Donny & Marie Show became a hit throughout the world. The Osmond Family Christmas shows became an annuity for years.

CHAPTER FOUR

Jimmy had the first gold record for the family in Japan, singing in Japanese. He also had a major hit in England called 'Long-Haired Lover from Liverpool.' Marie's personal career took off with her first hit record 'Paper Roses.' Marie also had hit after hit in her repertoire. Donny became a major teen idol, setting his personal career in motion, which caused not only hysteria to emerge, but Paul McCartney said it created mania, which are two very different reactions.

So, on and on we went, trying to reinvent ourselves along the way and remain commercial enough to keep the career moving forward.

The last performance we as the Osmond Brothers did, had been on our sister Marie's 60th birthday on the TV show called 'The Talk.' It was in October 2019 when the original lineup of Alan, Wayne, Jay, and I performed our last song together, which brother Alan wrote, called 'The Last Chapter.' As Marie watched us sing the song, she became emotional, and tears began to fall. Then Donny surprised everyone as he walked on stage. No one knew he was going to come in—not even the show's producer. We were all together for that one last show. The emotions were very raw among us.

Since then, there have been a lot of health issues the different siblings have had to go through. Brother Alan has multiple sclerosis, although his motto is 'I may have MS but MS does not have me.'

Wayne, who we have since lost in January 2025, had brain cancer, which robbed him of his hearing and then he suffered from two strokes.

Our little brother Jimmy suffered a major stroke while performing on stage in a pantomime in England on 27th December 2018. This was a devastating shock for the family. He no longer performs on stage, but he continues to do well and is enjoying a quieter life now with his family and has taken up painting again—he always had an amazing talent as an artist.

Jay continues to do various projects and now lives in Branson.

Brother Donny never stops; he has endless energy! He has a residency at Harrahs in Las Vegas and travels the world to sell-out audiences, singing all his hit records.

Marie also still performs occasionally, performing to sell-out Christmas shows and is a spokesperson for many major products around the world. Marie is also enjoying her time now as a grandma.

I, myself, have diabetes, heart issues, kidney issues, and bipolar tendencies that keep the doctors busy tending to my problems.

Just before going on Mary's and my mission in April 2023, Mary and I had a routine medical. The doctors told me I was a dead man walking and needed to have six stents put into my heart. Before the medical I was feeling fine and didn't know I had any issues. But the operation went well and I am grateful to Dr Michael Codiga—he truly is the only doctor in my life who has taken the time to check me out in all areas of my health.

I had wanted to keep this private but a TV station had called the hospital asking questions so this was posted on my social media.

'Rumors have been spreading that Merrill was hospitalized today with heart issues. To set the record straight, because of the advice of his Dr and health professionals, Merrill was advised to have stents fitted into his heart as a precaution. This has been done today and Merrill would like everyone to know he is feeling fine and should be released to go back home tomorrow.'

Loving each other was what we were brought up to do and believe by our family-oriented, moral, and highly aspirational parents. My mother's motto was in Latin, called 'Petimus Altiora,' which means 'We seek after higher things.'

CHAPTER FOUR

My mother had an enormous appetite for reading and learning; she encouraged us to read from the best books and learn from the best teachers, always doing our best to keep and maintain good standards. To be good Christians and follow the Lord's path always.

Both she and her father came from strong pioneering backgrounds, and the need to work hard and strive has been deeply ingrained into our souls. In the late 1800s, my paternal great-grandfather was asked to organize a settlement in Star Valley, Wyoming.

That first harsh winter, he, his wife, and their children had to live in a dugout on the side of a mountain. They experienced crop failure and starvation. Undeterred, my great-grandfather struggled on, even trading supplies with Indians, and working as a mail carrier through some of the most treacherous winters in Wyoming history, to provide for his family.

In the process, he became the first magistrate, judge, state senator, and a strong spiritual leader in that community. Life didn't get much easier for his son, my grandfather, who, as a husband and father himself, was helping his neighbor move firewood down from the mountains one day when the neighbor's mule became stuck in the mud. Grandfather hitched his own team of horses to the mule to pull him out. In the process, his favorite horse, Bird, kicked my grandfather hard, lacerating his liver. At the age of 27, he died that same day, November 24, 1917, in the service of others.

He left my sweet, widowed grandmother, Laverna, to raise their children herself. One of these was my father, George, who had been born the month before and was exactly five weeks old at the time. Afterwards, Laverna, who was left struggling to support herself and her family, moved them constantly. They moved from Star Valley, Wyoming, to Burley, Idaho, then to Ogden, Utah, Los Angeles, and San Diego, before returning to Wyoming.

In his journal, my father wrote, 'In San Diego, we lived on the edge of a canyon, where there were a lot of trees. We had a dog named Mickey that our neighbor did not like very well. One day he fed him some food with ground glass in it, and we all watched him die.'

In another entry, he records helping his elder brothers, Roland and Ralph, with their paper deliveries, writing, 'I always helped them. At three o'clock every morning we were folding papers on the street corner. One morning we looked up and I watched a big plane in the sky crash into a smaller plane. The big plane spun around in a circle and then plunged into the canyon.'

It was all deeply unsettling for my sensitive father, whose childhood traumas went on to frame his whole life. Sadly, things did not improve for him when his mother eventually remarried a man who partly owned a bakery in Los Angeles. This man was not very good at showing his feelings, so he compensated for his awkwardness by teasing and playing practical jokes on people.

One time, Father remembered, he was riding with him to Tijuana in Mexico. At the border, his stepfather thought it would be funny to tell the guards, whom he knew, that George had been drinking constantly. They drew a line on the floor and made him walk to test his sobriety. Although it was harmless fun, it was terrifying and humiliating for my father, who became the regular target of family jokes. Another time, his cousin Helen locked him in a pigeon coop, where he remained trapped for the rest of the day.

His stepfather was a gambler and took chances on several money-making enterprises, which turned out to be unsuccessful. One of these was gold mining, and when the vein ran out, he seemed to suffer a breakdown and lose touch with reality. In an attempt to keep her family together, Laverna left him and moved back to

CHAPTER FOUR

Wyoming, where she took a job as a housekeeper for a widower with five children of his own.

She kept busy, not just running the household, but milking his cows as well. She sent her older sons to live with relatives; only Father stayed there with her and the five motherless children. After a couple of years, Laverna married the widower, but Father and his new stepfather never got along. By the time he was 15, his stepfather had thrown him out of the house, and our father started supporting himself by doing odd jobs. His poor situation did not stop him from graduating from Star Valley High School in 1936.

Afterwards, a friend talked him into joining the Civilian Conservation Corps, as his two older brothers had done before him. The CCC, or C.C.C., as it was known, was for single men between the ages of 18 and 25 to enlist in work programs to improve America's public lands, forests, and parks. For many, a roof over their heads, a bed, and three meals a day was all the encouragement they needed to join.

For my father, it became a recipe for his difficult nomadic life, and he was welcomed into the camp that his brother Ralph had recently left. Ralph had been a cook there and had also represented the camp in boxing, which earned him a good reputation. I think it's probably fair to say that my father benefited from Ralph's legacy. His assigned role was not to dig ditches or fight fires, but to take charge of the recreation room, where he spent his time racking pool balls and cleaning up the place.

He was never one to waste his spare time, so he learned to play the guitar and sing a few songs. He bought a little recording machine. Then he was given a new assignment, serving the commissioned officers their meals and taking care of the division's office. There he learned to type and do a little shorthand. Some years before, Father had injured his back in an accident. It was at the CCC that he discovered he needed surgery to correct the damage to his spine. He was sent to Cheyenne for the operation, and there they removed his tonsils at the same time. As you can imagine, his recovery was rough and lonely.

When America became involved in World War II, his subsequent assignment meant that he was sent to England, where he was stationed at a shipyard supply depot. Working there, he witnessed many bombings and large-scale destruction, which didn't help his delicate nerves. Once his war was over, he was relieved of duty and returned home suffering from post-traumatic stress disorder. There was no treatment or therapy available back then as there is now.

Because he was also struggling with self-esteem and abandonment issues, he wasn't coping well and pleaded with God for relief from the painful memories that haunted him. Unable to stop thinking about events from the past, he felt fearful and nervous, and for years he suffered from bad dreams.

I purposely tell this sad chapter in our history because it goes a long way in explaining why my father became the forceful Osmond patriarch that he was. There was no denying that at times he was a stern and relentless taskmaster who encouraged us to push ourselves to the limit to succeed in the entertainment industry. He wanted to build a comfortable, secure future for his family, which hadn't been possible in his own impoverished, traumatic past.

We all had our daily farm and household chores and responsibilities from the moment we were awakened by Alan playing reveille on the trumpet. Together, we marched to breakfast to the sound of our mother's piano playing. If you didn't get your chores done, there were consequences. At times, I was taken outside by my father to pick my own willow for him to use to spank me when I did something wrong. It sounds really cruel, but I think we have to remember that you cannot always make judgments about the past from a different place and time.

CHAPTER FOUR

Growing up, my father did not have a positive father figure, so he had no role model. There is no doubt in my mind that his actions were born out of love and his innate desire for us to thrive and survive as a family.

I believe that sometimes rigid discipline had one definite advantage. With so many young boys and so many different personalities living under one roof, you might expect more than a few physical fights to break out between us over the years, but I honestly can't remember any—not one.

We were encouraged to practice boxing, though, to defend ourselves from bullies in the outside world. Behind our home was a reform school, and occasionally we had a few clashes with the boys going to school there.

As a shy middle child in our large family, I didn't seek confrontation or handle stress well. I was named the 'Man with the Oranges' by my maternal grandfather Davis because if I walked into a room with a bag full of them, I would hand them out to everyone there before taking one myself.

I also had the nickname of 'Melody' and 'Bear.' Melody came from my little canary that I loved so much. Bear, which stuck, came from Wayne. For some reason, he never pronounced the name Merrill very well; it always came out as 'Mirror' at first. Eventually that became 'Bear' and was adopted by my whole family. I liked it because I've always loved giving and receiving great big bear hugs. 'Black Bear' came later for much fewer flattering reasons, as you will discover.

Just before our father died at age 90 in 2007, he called me to his bedside. Through all our lives, from us being little children at our Friday night dinners to that moment, he had been a strong believer that the family that played together stayed together. He didn't mean just musical instruments either. Nothing changed his attitude even in his final days, and he wanted me to promise him something.

I'll never forget the moment my father leaned in close and whispered something into my ear that would shape the course of my entire life. He told me I was the peacemaker of our family. Not just a passing role—but a divine responsibility. He said, "It's up to you to help keep everyone happy… to keep the spirit strong in our home."

Those words settled into me like a sacred assignment.

In my journal, I later wrote that he told me something even deeper: "You need to keep our family strong in the gospel. Don't let anyone from the outside get in and cause problems." He didn't mean that with suspicion or fear—but with a plea for protection. For unity. He knew the forces that would try to divide us. He knew how easily fame, fortune, or even just fatigue could chip away at the bonds of faith and family.

From that moment forward, I carried that with me. Whether I was on a stage, in a boardroom, or sitting around the dinner table with my brothers and sisters, I often felt that quiet whisper echoing in my heart. Be the peacemaker. Hold the line. Protect the family. Keep the light of the gospel burning.

And even when I stumbled—and I certainly have—I never stopped trying.

My mother had been the first to recognize me as the peacemaker of the family years before, and it is a role that I have always taken very seriously. Never in a billion years did I ever think that the time would come when I would not be able to do that.

Chapter Five

FAME AND FORTUNE

As exciting as the 60s was for the Osmonds, when our career started taking off, it certainly wasn't an easy decade. We were desperately trying to find our niche in the entertainment world.

Just imagine for a minute, having to learn to ice skate within a week to perform live on an ice stage in front of millions of people on the Andy Williams TV show. Then it was learning to play piano, then tap dancing on top of them.

Somehow, we always took the view that, whatever the challenge, we could do it. Nothing was impossible. The old motto was 'the show must go on.' Come heck or high water. I had mentioned earlier that we were known as the 'One Take Osmonds.' If there was a little mistake, we would always smile and work as a team to correct it within seconds. But boy, did it take some blood, sweat, and tears.

By the end of the week, practicing relentlessly and rehearsing in the studios, we would work into the early hours to perfect it. It was truly amazing what we were able to achieve in one week if we set our minds to it.

Our efforts paid off because there was something about the 70s that was entirely different from the 60s. Early in 1971, when

I was just 17 years old, my family was living in Arleta, California. We had several homes throughout our childhood, including our favorite cabin retreat in Huntsville, Utah. We were able to camp out, go fishing, have family barbecues, and when winter came, we took our sleds, snowboards, and skis and had fun racing down the snow-covered mountains.

Every week, my brothers and I were challenged to perform something new on Andy's show. If we didn't, we didn't get invited back. We were constantly under pressure to come up with something new and different, yet keep the show professionally polished at all times. My memory of the day we learned that Peggy Fleming would appear on the Christmas show is quite vivid. In the ice-skating world, Peggy was the world champion. We were told that the entire stage would be covered in ice. If we did not know how to ice skate, we would not be invited to participate in the show.

Once again, we accepted the challenge. Having only four days to pull this off, and make it look extremely professional, was a huge challenge for us. Our father purchased us all brand new ice skates, arranged for us to use an ice skating rink after hours and hired a professional to teach us how to skate. The Christmas show aired across the country—not only did we do all of the fancy flips but we also held fireworks in our hands while we did our jumps and turns. The amazing part of this was The Ice Capades liked our show so much that they invited us to tour with them across the country. After the show was taped, all of our feet were bleeding and we were in so much pain, so we gathered around a large barrel and dumped our ice skates into the flames. Despite the pain, we felt a sense of accomplishment. Our dedication and hard work had paid off and we were thrilled and honored to be invited to tour with The Ice Capades. The experience taught us the value of perseverance and teamwork and we will always cherish

CHAPTER FIVE

the memories of that unforgettable Christmas show. But we never did any more ice skating!

Loving the whole rock 'n' roll scene and feeling that we were capable of writing and recording songs that could make it on the radio really excited us. I remember trying to make the decision to leave The Andy Williams Show and have the faith to move into a new part of the music business.

Our manager at that time was Andy Williams' brother, Don. Perhaps unsurprisingly then, there was a tremendous amount of stress put on us to never leave Andy. Don said that the amount of exposure we were getting throughout the world would end, and all the hard work we had done to get that opportunity from Andy would have been in vain as it would destroy our career. But there was something inside that was driving us to move forward.

Without really knowing the steps that it would take to get onto the pop music scene, we accepted the offer to become regular guests on the Jerry Lewis show, playing Las Vegas with artists like Nancy Sinatra, Phyllis Diller, and Pat Boone. Then in 1969, we again signed up to appear on The Andy Williams Show for another year.

But the itch to move forward into the record business was overpowering, and the opportunity to remain on weekly television was tempting. In 1970, we met a man by the name of Mike Curb, who was president of MGM Records. He believed in us enough to give us our big recording break.

I remember so well the day when all the siblings gathered around the radio listening to the Casey Kasem countdown show. Every week, our new single 'One Bad Apple' would climb the charts. Two months later, in February 1971, we were all stunned to learn that it had reached number one on the US Billboard Hot 100 charts. Just as a side note, that song had originally been written with The Jackson 5 in mind, but they passed on it.

When Casey said, 'Now, the number one song in America is by the Osmonds: 'One Bad Apple,' the excitement in our household hit fever pitch. We were screaming, yelling, dancing, and running around the house. We just could not believe it. When the decision was made to leave The Andy Williams Show, our manager said that we were too clean-cut to ever be accepted in the entertainment industry. Well, his prediction was extremely incorrect.

Our song remained in the charts for five whole weeks, and before we knew it, we had our first gold album. Then came offers for us to start doing concert appearances around the globe. We did not realize at the time that our records would be distributed throughout the world. One of the networks asked us to produce our first TV special called The Osmond Brothers Show, all thanks to a song that was predicted never to be a hit record.

I will never forget the memory of the time when we recorded that song. The producer, Rick Hall from the Fame Studios in Muscle Shoals, Alabama, picked Donny and myself to sing the leads. When I stepped up to the microphone that day, I literally became physically sick. I never told anyone that I was throwing up in the bathroom throughout the day because of the anxiety. But somehow, I managed to control my nerves and sang my heart out. I gave it everything I had.

Rick Hall, who Mike Curb chose to be the producer, was known industry-wide as the father of Muscle Shoals music; his influence was felt in both country and soul music. He had helped to develop the careers of the king and queen of soul, Otis Redding and Aretha Franklin.

Being a very shy and intimidated young guy, being chosen to be the lead singer of The Osmonds truly freaked me out. What a double-edged sword that turned out to be.

On the one hand, I felt enormously grateful to have my talent recognized by Rick Hall, but when Rick lined up Alan, Wayne, Jay, and myself to audition for the song, and I was the one he chose, it hurt my heart. Each one of them had incredible voices. But destiny had pointed its finger at me now.

My anxiety levels were soaring off the scale because from that moment on, the fever pitch surrounding the Osmonds began to escalate on both sides of the Atlantic. If I had feared making mistakes before, that fear now multiplied 100 times over.

In the same year that we had our success with One Bad Apple, the original Osmond Quartet expanded when Donny joined Alan, Wayne, Jay, and myself as a full-time member. The four originals had now become five.

During our time walking the streets of Disneyland, Donny had only been a toddler. But it was always assumed that he would join us one day. Our mother made him identical outfits—trousers, shirts, and bowties—to wear with the rest of us.

But then none of us knew the power and excitement that Donny would bring to the stage. My brother Donny had appeared on The Andy Williams Show when he was around five years old, but he wasn't a regular. Whenever he did appear, though, our little brother stole the show. His face was on every teen magazine.

By 13, like the rest of us, he had learned all the instruments that his brothers were playing. Donny seemed to gravitate to the piano. He also learned to play the organ, a little banjo, saxophone, and was challenged to even play the drums. But what I was always amazed at was his natural ability to tap dance with the rest of us.

Almost overnight, Donny became a heartthrob to young teenage girls everywhere he went. The high-pitched screams for him were almost deafening. For the first time, in May 1971, we appeared on a concert stage in Cleveland, Ohio, as the top-billed performers. We were no longer an opening and supporting act. Before we knew it, we were embarking on a very successful coast-to-coast tour of the

United States, appearing in 48 cities from July that year through September.

Donny had also embarked on a solo career with Sweet and Innocent and Go Away Little Girl. Again, his picture would be seen on the front cover of magazines throughout the whole world. Because of his personal attraction to fans, concert after concert would be sold out. Knowing my brother, like I do, he was a very modest and humble little guy, and all the attention embarrassed him at times. Donny was a team worker. He had been taught, like the rest of us, to keep our egos and pride in check.

By the end of 1971, the Osmonds had sold more records in a single year than any other group, including The Beatles. Serious amounts of dollars had begun rolling in, in the millions. Not just from record sales, but from concert tours, songwriting royalties, and merchandising.

My family and I have felt welcomed in countries around the world, whether through the TV shows we did or the thousands of records we recorded and sold.

On May 19, 1972, we made our first trip as a family to England. Our records had not yet been as popular there as they were in the United States. But we wanted to go to England because our mother wanted to discover more about our ancestors so she could start doing genealogy. Genealogy is encouraged by our church to find links that bind families together.

Important family records brought back to America in the 19th century had been damaged in a fire, and our family tree lacked necessary details.

Fire had also caused us another pain later in our lives. A couple of years after we had returned from England, a large folder of songs that Alan, Wayne and myself had written for an original album called The Plan burnt up in our hotel room in Memphis, Tennessee.

CHAPTER FIVE

It was a couple of years' worth of hard work, and for some reason, we never had a backup copy but we knew we would write it again.

The three of us would go into different rooms and we would write the melody and lyrics and then come in and listen to what we had done; we were always very critical of each other, which was good as we were all perfectionists. We would then toss out the things we didn't like and keep what we felt was right. The three of us worked hours and hours this way, just writing together.

This album was a change of direction and very important to us and we had put everything into it. It was like The Beatles' White Album was to them. It consisted of our religious beliefs told in a very abstract way. We had envisioned very broad styles of music to put across in a very commercial and contemporary album.

The album was not a popular conversation amongst our record company. We were right in the middle of our career. The last thing the record company wanted was to have a concept album come out that would change the sound and format of the hit records we were having.

Obviously, we were extremely discouraged and wondered if we should even rewrite it again, but, we did, and I still believe it was our best work. 'Let Me In,' 'Before the Beginning,' and 'Goin' Home' were all very well received by the fans and still are today.

On one occasion, we had been asked to appear in a Royal Gala at the London Palladium. It was being staged by the British TV channel ATV to raise funds for the British Olympic Team Appeal and watching us from the Royal Box would be Her Majesty the Queen and the Duke of Edinburgh, Prince Philip. We as a family, would often joke about meeting the Queen someday, but we hadn't really expected that to happen.

I remember the show very well. I don't know about the rest of the guys, but I was extremely nervous. There was a moment on stage that could have been disastrous when Donny's microphone suddenly went dead. Fortunately, our quick-thinking brother Wayne realized what had happened and switched microphones with him before it was his turn to sing. Our years of practiced teamwork went into action; no one in the audience even noticed.

Then came the moment we met Her Royal Highness. We were all backstage lined up with the other entertainers that were on the show. There was protocol that had to be followed. You could not speak to the Queen unless she spoke to you, and you could never reach out to shake her hand unless she wanted to shake yours.

When the Queen began to shake our mother's hand, my mother reached in her purse and gave her a Book of Mormon. The security went nuts. Her Majesty and our mother really hit it off at that moment. The two of them spent quite a bit of time talking about God and family. We were told Her Majesty kept that book in her personal library for years.

At that time in our career, the British fans had recognized us on the streets of London after seeing us on television but it was by no means on the same scale as it was in the United States. This allowed us to spend a couple of days indulging in a whirlwind sightseeing and shopping tour. My journal talks about how we went to Buckingham Palace, Big Ben, and the Houses of Parliament.

That opportunity stopped the next time we came back to England. I'll never forget the screams from thousands of girls in the audience at our concert. We performed at the Rainbow Theatre in Finsbury Park in November 1972.

DJ Tony Prince, who worked for Radio Luxembourg, was a good friend to the Osmonds and wrote this following article in 1975.

The Osmonds' 1975 visit was planned like a military maneuver and even the family didn't know which route we were taking.

CHAPTER FIVE

We were informed that we were to depart from Liverpool's Lime Street station but in fact we were all taken by surprise when we realized that our coach was driving away from the city center. For a few minutes the whole entourage bated their breath hoping against hope that the journey to Scotland wasn't to be made by road. Then suddenly we stopped at a small railway station, and all piled out onto the platform which was barely long enough to hold us all. The station master must have been one of the few people who knew that the Osmonds were to actually use his station. Somebody had leaked the news and dozens of lucky fans stood around chatting excitedly to their heroes while each of them received autographs. Finally the Liverpool-Glasgow express pulled into our station. Normally the train shot through at 100 miles per hour but this time the residents around the area saw it stop for the very first time to collect its cargo of talent. We had a whole coach to ourselves and we actually filled it—that's how many people were on this tour! Snacks and 7Up were served as the engine whizzed us northwards. The same thing happened in Glasgow—we stopped at an unscheduled station just before the City.

This time there were a good hundred fans 'in the know.' A new coach waited, its engine running, its driver excited about his job today as he'd ever been. As usual the boys found time to say hello to everyone before we finally urged them aboard. Glasgow is always an exciting audience and it seems what Alan predicted was true, 'The fans will grow up with us.'

Later that night, after we had escaped the enthusiastic fans and re-entered our hotel, we all got together for a farewell meal. Most of the boys had gone to bed and I sat chatting *to Mr and Mrs Osmond, who at last found time to relax. A young woman came into the room with a small girl who we were told was her younger sister who wanted nothing more in life than to meet Donny. We were just about to explain that Donny had retired when Donny walked into the room. Sleeping in hotels during an Osmond tour is not always easy, especially if you are an Osmond and have thousands of fans calling out your name beneath your window.*

This then was the young girl's chance of a lifetime! The older sister told Donny her younger sister's name and Donny said 'hi' and told her he was pleased to meet her. All the little girl could do was look at Donny, not two feet away, and cry!

After returning home to Utah from that trip to England, our popularity began quickly soaring in the UK as well as the United States. The royal TV gala, where we performed for Her Majesty, finally aired and it obviously had a huge effect on our career.

Our song Down by the Lazy River hit the UK charts with a lot of excitement. Donny's song Puppy Love was then released, which topped the charts that summer, and he had another success with the song Too Young.

Things quickly changed with our record label, Polydor, who worked in conjunction with MGM, decided that we needed to return to London quickly. Polydor sent their top executive, Roger Holt, to Las Vegas to watch us perform at Caesar's Palace.

Our song Crazy Horses was already climbing the charts in the United States. Once again, both record labels worried that the heavier style of music might not be the right mix for the UK fans. But they didn't need to worry—it took off.

Polydor Records and their public relations machine went into overdrive. Radio Luxembourg was playing our music constantly for

CHAPTER FIVE

a week before we arrived back in Britain. When we touched down at Heathrow Airport, it was a major shock to see thousands of screaming, banner-waving girls waiting to greet us.

It was a very different reception from the previous one, and it made headlines in the next day's newspapers. Some even estimated that as many as 12,000 young fans, who they labeled 'screaming teeny boppers,' had traveled to be there.

During one of the concerts, all our training to harmonize with perfect pitch, went out of the door. I, for one, could not hear myself sing, let alone try to find harmony to a chord that first night at the Rainbow Theatre.

Camera crews were everywhere, and flashbulbs were popping and snapping continually. It was truly overwhelming. Scotland Yard was there to make sure we had a rapid exit. They even arranged to have us get into a getaway milk truck.

Our tour manager, Ed Leffler, who had previously worked for The Beatles, knew all the tricks of the trade. We were dressed in numerous disguises, including London Bobby outfits, to get around.

We were ushered into bread vans and all sorts of vehicles, including ambulances, fire trucks, and police trucks to get past the overwhelming gathered fans. I had always wondered what would happen if they did catch us. I'm truly serious, it was scary.

We stayed at the Churchill Hotel, hiding away behind lace curtains in our rooms. This was just the start of us living in a bubble that became impossible for us to burst out of. Our normal lifestyle had now taken on an extreme, even terrifying, aspect.

While being scared for ourselves at times, we also worried constantly about the fans and their own safety amidst the chaotic scenes going on. The hotel was surrounded by thousands of fans. Being raised, as we had been, to want to not only shake someone's hand but even give them a hug complicated things with Scotland

Yard. The last thing they wanted was to have mobs of people gathered in areas where traffic jams could occur.

We finally negotiated with Scotland Yard that 15-minute intervals would occur where we would all step out onto the balcony and wave. Well, that didn't work. When we walked out, hundreds of girls ran across the street and, in some cases, walked on top of cars to get to our side of the street. I'll never forget the scene. In fact, it's etched into my mind when a few Rolls-Royces and Bentleys had their roofs bent in by the bodies stomping on top of their cars.

On another occasion, when flying into England, the pilot of our plane was told that because he was carrying the Osmonds on board, his landing privileges had been withdrawn and we were being diverted to the airport in Manchester. Oh boy, the people on board were so mad. I can't even imagine how upset they must have been.

Another memory that will always stick in my brain was when Scotland Yard ordered the fire department to spray hoses of water into the crowds so we could get our cars out of the garage at the hotel.

There was a BBC documentary that aired showing the hysteria that was going on. They called it Osmond Mania. They showed at least ten to 15 girls scaling the outside of the hotel to try to get access to our bedroom windows. Amidst all the chaos, three police officers were hit over the head with bottles. A fireman was stabbed, and axes were used to try to break down doors to enter the hotel.

I wrote in my journal, 'There is no way to go outside the hotel. I guess it's pizza and home movies for us.' Outside, there was a constant chorus of fans yelling, 'We want the Osmonds! We want the Osmonds!' Again, I cannot imagine what the people staying at that hotel were thinking. This was to be our life for many years to come.

Chapter Six

MARY, MY DARLIN'

In my youth, I used to pray day and night that I would find my sweetheart. At 20 years old, I wrote in my journal: 'Heavenly Father, please lead me to the one I can spend my life with, someone who knows and understands the meaning of a forever family. The temptations of the flesh are so great. Please help me find this lady worthy to be the wife and mother to the family we can one day bring into this world.'

Living by our religious beliefs as a member of The Church of Jesus Christ of Latter-day Saints, I worked very hard to keep my moral compass in check. Having enormous popularity at 20 years old meant that there were plenty of girls only too willing to date an Osmond brother.

With several hit records on the charts and every concert selling out, our family name carried quite an attraction, and temptation really was everywhere. I remember one day I was walking through the Detroit airport when I heard some screams. I looked around, then I was being attacked by a few gals who ripped my shirt completely off. I literally had to board the plane without a shirt. The looks I got were quite embarrassing, to say the least.

Everywhere my brothers and I would go, the paparazzi would always be there, hoping to find some picture with the opposite sex hanging onto us, trying to show the vulnerability and moral weakness a young teenager could have.

This might even shock those of you reading this, but I only dated three times before I met my wife. Another revelation that I rarely speak about but thought it would be interesting for the reader is that I actually had kissing lessons. I had seen it in action, obviously, and there seemed to be a technique, but I sure wasn't schooled in it.

One day I was sitting in the dentist's chair getting a tooth fixed when a little conversation started to happen with the dentist about dating the right girl and how to know when to kiss them. It was actually pretty funny. It was a lot funnier because I had laughing gas over my nose at the time. Anyway, his nurse was there listening to the whole conversation. When the dentist was done, and I started to walk out the door, this nurse came up to me and said, 'Hey, if you want to know how to kiss, I can show you how.' It was a very strange offer, but I accepted the invitation.

She said, 'When the dentist leaves to go home, come to the back door, and I'll let you in. Just sit in the dentist chair, and I'll lower the seat and show you all the different techniques.'

Well, to make a long story short, years later when I started dating Mary, she told me I was the best kisser she had ever kissed. Funny how life prepares you in the most unexpected ways.

A few years later, in 1973, a friend of mine set up a date without telling me with the reigning Miss California. The poor girl drove for hundreds of miles all the way down from the golden state to Utah only to be badly let down. I couldn't go on a date with her because another friend who had been dating my brother, Alan, had already set me up on a blind date with a former cheerleader, Mary Carlson.

CHAPTER SIX

The day I met Mary was interesting. She was a little gal that was tough and down to earth. She had an extreme love and compassion about her that just radiated from her. She still does.

At the time of the date, there was a very important meeting I needed to attend at Robert Redford's restaurant at Sundance Ski Resort. I guess Mary knew many of our songs but wasn't interested in going out. She had this mindset thinking she'd be going out with a stuck-up and egotistic entertainer. But then she thought, 'Hmm, if I go out with him to Robert Redford's restaurant (which she loved), I'll just order the biggest and most expensive dinner possible. That would be worth it!'

When we saw each other for the first time, though, something truly magical occurred. It was like we had known each other our whole lives. I knew right then and there that she would be my wife. We continued to date, and our relationship got serious—so serious that our manager, agent, and public relations guru were all trying to discourage me from dating her. The reason was simple: if I were to get married, there would be a dip in interest from the fans to buy the records or come to the concerts. The lead singer getting married could seriously damage our momentum in the record industry.

These individuals even started telling my father about their concerns. This made things even more problematic for me. The day came when Mary and I decided that we wanted to get married. I called my parents and said I needed to meet with them. We had this big conference table in one of our rooms. Sitting at the head of one end was my father. Sitting at the other end was me. On either side sat my mother and Mary. It only took a few seconds for me to simply say that I wanted to get married to this wonderful individual and that I wanted to get my father's blessings.

Oh boy, wrong maneuver! His answer was no and he followed it by saying, 'All she wants is your money.' But my mother just smiled and said, 'I think it's great.' Two very opposite comments. Well, that conversation lasted for about ten minutes, and we got up and left. My mother was my hero because she encouraged me to follow my heart, which I did. The marriage was on.

One of the funny stories Mary told me later was that one of her cousins went to the grocery store one day and bought some packets of Osmond bubble gum that contained cards with pictures of us all on. I guess it wasn't a very flattering picture of me with long hair and wearing a terrible-looking shirt. That was almost a turn-off for Mary.

But what seemed to change her opinion about wanting to go out with me was when I asked her to go to church with me. That shocked her. She could never imagine a stuck-up entertainer would want to go to church. At that church meeting, I was called and ordained to become a Melchizedek Priesthood holder in our church.

I remember on our third date we decided to go to dinner at one of our favorite restaurants in town. At that time, I didn't have my own car. When any of us wanted to go somewhere we had to check with our parents before we could take the family car.

Mary owned a little Pontiac Firebird that had a stick shift, four on the floor as they say. I had never used a clutch before but trying to be a macho man and impress her I offered to drive. Well, what a disaster that was. I would drive maybe 20 feet then stop, I'd start back up again, going another 20 feet and we would stop again. Mary was laughing so hard, it was embarrassing, it finally got to the point where out of sheer desperation, I begged her to please just drive. None of that mattered because that third date, we knew we were going to be buddies the rest of our lives.

When Donny, Marie and Jimmy needed a summer tutor, my mother asked Mary to step in and do that job. Mary was an amazing teacher and a well-educated person. That became an opportunity

CHAPTER SIX

for me to see her on a regular basis before I was leaving to head off on a long concert tour. Being separated from her that first time made me realize how much I truly cared for her. At the time she was away on vacation in Hawaii with her aunt. Somehow, I managed to track her down and we spent hours chatting on the phone. After the tour finished and I returned to Utah, I asked her to marry me. She had recently graduated from Brigham Young University with a degree in business education and had gotten her first job as a teacher. It was her dream job, and she was so excited about it. I proposed during her first week in the classroom and, incredibly, she said yes. I am still humbled to think that she was prepared to give it all up for a life with me that was never going to be easy by anyone's standards.

It was during this time that our family received a death threat from the Symbionese Liberation Army, a small American militant far left organization that was active between 1973 and 1975.

It was a very serious threat, and my every move was under surveillance by the police department. Mary also had to be carefully protected, and a police car was assigned to follow her around. Thrown into the spotlight herself because of her association with me, she too was at risk. Though it made her very nervous, it only strengthened our love for one another, and to be able to protect each other when times got bad.

We were married on September 17, 1973, at 11 in the morning at the Salt Lake City Temple. I was 20 and Mary was 22. I was the lead singer and the first performing Osmond to get married, so the paparazzi and every network channel were there in an attempt to get a scoop on that very special moment.

During our wedding ceremony that took place in the sealing room of the temple, only a few close family and friends attended. My father and mother along with brother Virl and Tommy who were the only ones out of the family that had a Temple Recommend. To enter the temple and become a part of that sacred experience, one must have a Temple Recommend. Our dear friend Paul H Dunn was the one who married us. Everyone else was waiting for us in the lobby afterwards.

Mary wore the most beautiful wedding dress. We had given each other our wedding rings. Her ring was constructed of two bands of white gold connected by an arch with a sparkling solitaire diamond on top.

She gave me a beautiful gold band with a diamond on top with an inscription inside that says something that only I can see. A message that will last throughout all eternity.

We celebrated our wedding breakfast at the Lion House, a building belonging to the church. And we were able to share our happiness with 200 invited family members and friends for this event. I was able to change into a navy double breasted, pinstriped suit and a shirt with a very large collar and tie, all very 70s!!

Outside the gates of the Temple where the paparazzi and about every network channel had gathered, there were also hundreds of people stood around those temple gates to get a glimpse or a picture of the two of us.

There were so many cameras going off that the Temple security told us that we would need to leave in separate cars and go through an underground tunnel, then meet up at a certain location. I was to wear a straw hat and sunglasses to disguise myself.

A big reception had been arranged for us by our friend Mike Curb at his home in Beverly Hills, California. A lot of very special friends and entertainers showed up but the ones I'll never forget were Richard and Karen Carpenter. They had always been good friends. They gave Mary and me the most beautiful silver platter

CHAPTER SIX

with an inscription on it. They put their names on the back of this platter—this is still in our home today.

Another reception was arranged for us in Heber city, Utah, Mary's birthplace. I remember the line being so long it went around the whole block. Mary and her family had the greatest reputation anyone could ever have in that little valley.

Our marriage began in a three-bedroom duplex. Even though we had a few million dollars of family money in the bank, Mary and I lived off a very small amount of money to pay rent and the necessities. And even though there wasn't a lot of money to spoil each other, we were the happiest couple on the planet.

We had always spoken about having a large family. We always wanted a house full of children and we did get our wish. First came Travis Merrill Osmond, born October 1975, followed by Justin Alan Osmond in March 1977. Then Shane George came in May 1979. Heather was born in September 1982 and our little Troy Dean, who we were destined to lose so young, was born November 1984. Then finally our little Sheila, who we adopted when she was just a baby, was born in July of 1986.

Even with two parents with hands on deck, a family of that size took a whole lot of work. There was also an additional care needed for our little boy Justin because of his severe hearing loss.

I was still entertaining throughout the world, and it required that I be gone for long periods of time. Mary was the hero. She took care of everything from nuts and bolts to changing hundreds of diapers, to taking the kids to school and back, and everything else you can imagine. At home, Mary imposed pretty strict household rules that had to be followed to the letter.

I didn't see Mary or the kids as often as I wanted to and every time I would leave for a trip, it became harder to leave.

Because of Mary's formal education she was able to manage to help with all the homework but because of my lack of a formal education, I couldn't help our kids very much even if I'd been home, I'd have no clue about the history or the math that they were studying.

But somehow, Mary did it all and somehow always managed to support me 100% as well—she still does today. She has never wanted to be in the limelight. She never had a desire to be on stage or to receive any kind of applause, she was just very content with being a wife, a mother and now a grandmother.

In her own way, Mary was kind of like a pioneer. She never had much as a child as her father died young from diabetes when she herself was only five years old. Suddenly widowed, her mother got all of her kids to work on the dairy farm, milking the cows and doing all the hard labor. Mary worked hard to save enough to put herself through a university education and become a teacher.

It wasn't easy being an Osmond wife in the crazy 70s. It took a very special person to embrace the intense challenges that always confronted her. But there was always one thing that Mary wanted to do and had never thought she would be able to do, and that was to travel. So I'm glad that I was able to give her that opportunity. But after our 50th year wedding anniversary, her desire is to now just stay home and visit the kids.

As a wife and a mother, Mary truly is the best thing that could've ever happened to me, but whether the same could be said of me is a question that only she can answer.

Every sibling has their own version of how things began. It's been interesting to read the many takes on our history. I am grateful I kept a detailed journal, but even more grateful that my wife Mary kept an even more thorough one.

Mary, the first to marry, has a powerful perspective. She has never wanted the spotlight, only to build a strong, grounded family.

CHAPTER SIX

Her values have been our anchor. Truthfully, had it not been for her steady hand and unwavering priorities, the entertainment industry could have easily pulled us away from what mattered more than hit records.

Chapter Seven

STARSTRUCK

Several years after the height of Beatlemania, I was lucky enough to be in Paris at the same time as Paul McCartney, someone I have always greatly admired, especially since the time the Osmonds first hit the UK in the early 1970s. I really am a big fan of his.

It was an unbelievably crazy time when Osmond mania was being compared to the Beatlemania experienced by John, Paul, George, and Ringo when they arrived in America.

For four weeks, we made the front pages of the national press, but not always for the reasons we might have wanted. Some newspapers really didn't like us, and they made no secret about it. We were heavily criticized by music journalists for being squeaky clean, plastic, and bubblegum.

Ringo Starr, one of the Beatles, also came out and blasted our music. We were obviously crushed by hearing his comments. During all of this craziness, it was Paul, who we had never met, that came to our defense. Totally unprompted, he made headlines telling our critics that they didn't know us, and they had not really listened to our music. He specifically noted our Plan album and how much he liked it.

To read all of this was a shock to us all because when a former Beatle defends you, people listen and take notice. Even the press and all the negative headlines and stories stopped overnight. His kindness really made us want to meet him. Though to be fair, that wasn't the only reason. I admired his voice, his ability to write the songs he did, the way he played his bass guitar, and, even more importantly, his overall great attitude.

Being very honest, it was an image that I wanted to copy. He really was, and still is, my musical idol to this day, and there is nothing I would love more than to perform a duet in concert with that man. So, if there's any chance you're reading this, brother Paul, and like the idea, please get in touch. Oh, what a day that could be!

Through Paul's people and the people that worked with us, a meeting was set up in the stunning art deco Four Seasons Hotel George V in the French capital. I'll never forget it—starstruck, waiting there, nervously poised for the big moment. My wife, Mary, was on my left-hand side, and my brother Donny was on my right.

The door to the meeting room began to open, and suddenly there was a loud scream from Paul's little daughter as she ran to grab hold of Donny. Seconds later, there was another sudden scream—this time from Mary, who also ran to get a hug from her Beatles idol, Paul!

Unless you were there, it's hard to describe just how thrilling that moment was. It had all the makings of a headline event—the kind paparazzi dream about. But the best part for me? Watching my sweet little wife meet her idol. The way her eyes lit up—it was like watching a dream come true right in front of me. It certainly made a change for the shoe to be on the other foot. Usually, it was Mary dealing with fans screaming after me and my brothers. It was so awesome to see Mary get so excited.

I have often wished the audience could see themselves the way I saw them. From the stage, I didn't just see the faces—I felt

CHAPTER SEVEN

hearts. The love, sincerity and pure gratitude that they radiated back to me was unlike anything else I have ever experienced. There were moments, mid-song, when I would catch someone's eyes filled with emotion or see families holding each other close, and I couldn't help but tear up. It wasn't just applause or admiration, it was something deeper. A sacred connection between souls. I wish they knew what that did to me. How it healed me, lifted me and reminded me why I kept going. Those were the moments that made all the sacrifices worth it.

I will never forget Tony Brainsby, one of the sharpest minds in public relations, who had worked not only with The Beatles but also with The Osmonds. He knew the ins and outs of the industry but more importantly he knew people. Tony understood me well enough to know that one of the greatest gifts I could ever dream of would be a bass guitar from Paul McCartney himself. Somehow he made that happen through his connections and sheer determination. I was stunned, humbled and speechless. To hold that bass in my hands—knowing where it had come from, who had touched it, who had played it—was more than just receiving an instrument. It was like receiving a piece of history... And a gesture of deep friendship I will never forget.

Throughout my 65-year career, I have played some of the most memorable concert venues imaginable. Those profound memories will never be forgotten. But the one venue that always sticks out as my favorite will be The Cavern, Liverpool, England. My personal passion to play the bass over the years hit the pinnacle when Paul McCartney gave me one of his basses. Paul ignited me to write, create and play that bass which gave me a solid foundation into music. To think that Paul started his career at The Cavern made a long-lasting impression on me. I've performed there a few times now and always feel honored to be invited back. Each time it was an amazing feeling.

When the management there asked me if I would put my name on a brick outside The Cavern, to be amongst some of the biggest names ever to perform there, I had to hold back the tears.

Crowds gathered as it was cemented into the wall. What an honor! Fans still go today and polish it, taking photos of it and posting them on my social media. I truly am humbled by this honor. To receive this brick means every bit as much to me as the star on the legendary Hollywood Walk of Fame that the Osmonds were honored with in 2003.

Then, they asked me to write a message on the wall that was right behind the stage The Beatles performed on. I remember staring at the many names. To add my name to theirs was a dream come true, I honestly didn't feel worthy.

I remember the moment I did a tribute to The Beatles there. I performed I Saw her Standing There, Let it Be, Hey Jude and Come Together, which is truly my favorite Beatles song. It was that bass riff that captured my imagination. The audience sang and swayed in unison as I was singing.

The last time I performed there was in April 2022 when the show we did was a 90-minute one with no interval. The place was sold out, the atmosphere was electric. What an emotional night for me. It was one of those shows that remains etched in my memories. This truly is one of the highlights of my career and one I will never forget.

I stayed in the hotel called A Hard Day's Night next door to The Cavern. It was arranged for me to stay in the Paul McCartney suite. I felt a blessed man that evening, the whole suite is dedicated to Paul. I remember I called my son Troy, who was so excited to hear about the memorabilia in the room and I promised I would bring him to experience The Cavern next time. Sadly, this never happened...

My band, Phil Hendriks, Dave Wallace and Pat Windebank, were all as excited as I was to play there again, we had so much fun during those shows there. The whole place was singing along and up dancing with us. It was my brother Jimmy's birthday so I decided to do a live feed and asked the audience to sing Happy Birthday to him followed by 'Long Haired Lover'! I know it meant a great deal to Jimmy that night to watch it all live. Liverpool has a special place in his heart due to his hit record, Long Haired Lover.

I don't honestly know if I will ever return to that cozy little place again, but I can now say I was there and truly had the time of my life! The iconic venue has enormous history in the music world. Brian Epstein saw The Beatles perform there and signed them. No more needs to be said.

Chapter Eight
REWRITTEN HISTORY

※

(This chapter deals with a sensitive issue that caused a lot of unneeded concern amongst many fans throughout the world. Because of the confusion it created, I decided to write about this and finally put to rest what became the rewritten history debacle.)

When my brother Jay first approached me around three or four years ago, he proposed an idea that he had already been working on involving a musical, telling the story about our family history. We were sat in the back of a car on our way to the airport after performing our last shows as Brothers in England. I told him, that while I thought it was a wonderful idea, I would have to pass because I had been contracted by Dixie State University College in Utah to do some production work, which would be taking most of my time.

But I wished him well. In that two-hour trip in the car, we talked about how he would deal with the content to make sure that the story would be an accurate reflection if the Osmond name was being used. We discussed the name of his musical. Jay and his wife, Karen, came up with the name, 'He Ain't Heavy, He's My Brother,' which would alleviate the worries of every Osmond wanting to ensure the history was correct.

It would be a musical from Jay's perspective without tying in the entire Osmond name and becoming the official story, and Jay agreed. Because the song 'He Ain't Heavy' had become a hit for the brothers, people would understand the meaning without putting the Osmond name front and center. I thought it was absolutely perfect and told him so, and I wished him well.

Then came a tremendous amount of drama. We found out that the name had been changed to 'The Osmonds: A New Musical by Jay Osmond'. That did get many of the siblings' attention. We then saw a press release from the producers of the musical, discussing the content of the musical, which was not flattering at all towards our father, Alan, and myself.

Even having seen that article, we knew that Jay might be dealing with a lot of pressure from not only the writers and producers but also the investors putting up the money. It was obvious that the name Osmond would probably be more appealing to the public than 'He Ain't Heavy.'

A few of the siblings wanted to read the script, but that request was denied. The siblings once again sensed that there was pressure being put on our brother, which he might need help resolving.

If there were music rights issues, those had to be dealt with. The publishers and writers had to give permission for that to happen. If logos or images were being used, that also had to be handled correctly. Every sibling knew that none of this would be happening if Jay were truly in control. Historically, whenever any member of the family engaged in movies or television shows depicting the Osmonds, we as a family were informed and had the opportunity to understand the content and express our opinions if there were differing views.

CHAPTER EIGHT

One thing I would say to anyone who may be reading this book is that I have never been jealous of my siblings. Not one. Not ever. It's always been 'all for one and one for all.' When news of Jay's musical had been steadily trickling onto social media and sadly dividing fans, I was accused online by a fan of being jealous of what Jay was doing. It's shameful because nothing could be further from the truth. That truly broke my heart, as that was 1000% not true.

One of our attorneys, named Rich Hill, who had been one of the attorneys for and a close friend of the Osmond family throughout the years, was asked to make a few phone calls. He never was paid for his services, by the way. But because of his relationship with the family, he wanted to help us try and figure things out.

He spoke to the producer of the musical and was assured that when the script was complete, certain members of the family could read it. He also called Mike Curb, who had been involved with our family for years and even owned the publishing and copyrights on a few of the songs we had written over the years. Rich was able to get a basic understanding that everything would be handled very legitimately and professionally. Then everything went quiet, and the musical was in the theaters.

Because of all of our busy schedules, none of the siblings were able to see the musical. However, we had reports, saw videos, and we heard a full audio recording. There were a few statements made that were incorrect. I was finally able to get a hold of my brother, and I asked him to please correct those untrue statements. He listened and agreed with me and said he would speak to the writers and producers and make those changes that same day.

I could go on trying to explain the frustration that some of us siblings went through at that time, but it's not important now and I don't want to say too much about it now.

It was made clear through social media that this story was how Jay saw the Osmonds' history and that for the first time he had his voice heard. The historical part was fine. Any sibling could tell their side of the story anywhere at any time; that would be their right to do so, but to say Jay never had a voice within the family for 60 years created such a stir within the fan base that fans were literally pitting themselves against each other, taking sides against certain siblings. That's when feelings started to get hurt.

The Osmond family, throughout our entire career, had never seen anything like this occur, ever. There were some who even questioned whether everything they had ever known or read about our family over the years was even true. Were we truly a united family?

I finally did respond and made a statement at one of my fan events in Las Vegas in April 2022, that if we, as a family, ever had a disagreement, we would internally work it out and it should never be discussed on social media. I concluded by saying, 'Just watch us. We solve our family problems internally.' I can honestly say those concerns and disagreements have now been resolved.

What none of us knew was that when our attorney started inquiring about the legal aspects of our music, image, and likeness, Jay was told by the producers to remain quiet and to even lawyer up. Then, Jay told us he had been told by someone outside the family, we were about to sue him. The truth is that would never happen within our family. The love we have for each other, despite occasional disagreements, would always be settled in a loving way. I can now see that Jay was in a terrible predicament, being wrongly informed by someone we were going to sue him and why he was advised to stay away from any conversation with his family. It was a complete lie, which Jay also now knows. We weren't going to sue him. It went crazy on social media, fans were taking sides, this had never happened before, and it was a sad situation that could've been avoided.

We pray that those who literally turned bitter towards any Osmond sibling over this problem will hopefully remember the good things that we as a family did together. Remember how you might have felt when you heard a certain song that helped you get through some tough times. Remember that every family has issues—problems that sometimes will never resolve themselves. But the Osmonds have and will continue to do so as long as we are still on this planet.

The statement about Jay not having a voice is incorrect. Jay was the one who was asked by the family to oversee the movie 'Side by Side: The True Story of Our Family.' He was the one who corrected the scripts to ensure everything was exactly as it was supposed to be. He remained on site as the entire movie was produced to again ensure that everything was correct.

Jay was also the one who oversaw all the concert segments of the Donny & Marie Shows, 'A Little Bit Country, A Little Bit Rock 'n' Roll.' He chose the music and choreographed the dance steps for Donny and Marie. Brother Jay was always there in a family circle where we made family decisions. Jay voted like the rest of us to do the projects that we did, including building our television studio in Orem, Utah. Jay's voice was always heard when we put our concert show rundowns together. I could go on but suffice it to say my brother did have a voice then and continues to have a voice now.

How all that propaganda of him not having a voice started is still a dilemma for many of us. Every sibling wanted Jay to succeed with his musical, but the Osmond brand needed to be protected as we had always done through our entire career. That was the only thing that created the tension, and we truly believe our brother had a tremendous amount of stress and pressure placed upon him to put the best spin on the musical that could be done. That's why 'The Osmonds, a New Musical' was used instead of 'He Ain't Heavy, He's My Brother.'

Just to set the record straight as to who wrote the music to our repertoire, Alan, Wayne, and I are the ones who wrote the songs. This is all documented, on the records, and published. I'm not sure why this question keeps coming up but it does. There were times when our brother Jay occasionally would come in and play drums to help enhance certain songs, but he didn't write the songs. Jay's input was valuable during songs like Hold her Tight and My Drum, but every note, every word, every concept where a song is created, it came from Alan, Wayne and myself.

Together the three of us sat there, hour after hour after hour writing songs. When a song is written it's the lyrics, and a bridge and a verse and a chorus and a fade. There is a lot to do putting it all together and then making it commercial to go out on the radio.

Even though brother Jay wasn't a writer, we split things financially four ways which means that he gets the same royalties today as we do for the writing, even though he wasn't a writer.

Having said that, Alan, Wayne and myself have never received a dime in royalties for our music used in Jay's musical…

Chapter Nine

CLOSE SHAVES AND TESTING TIMES

～※～

My father suffered with anxiety and depression his whole life. Back in his day, the subject was rarely—if ever—talked about. There were no real treatments, no proper understanding and certainly nothing available to help those who struggled with what we now recognize as bipolar disorder.

As I look back on how he handled it all, I am honestly in awe. He bore a silent burden with such strength and somehow carried on without the benefit of any medication or support system that could truly understand him.

That same DNA was passed down to me. I have suffered greatly with many of the same battles he faced. Yet, understanding what he endured helps me realize I am not alone, and that what he carried in silence, I now carry with awareness and hopefully healing.

Throughout the pages of my journal and even more so in my wife's detailed entries—a clear pattern began to emerge, waves of extreme highs followed by crushing lows. The highs brought with them a flood of creative energy, moments where ideas poured out of me faster than I could capture them Those were the times I felt invincible, inspired, even prophetic in some strange way.

But the lows... those were something else entirely. They took me to places I never want to return to. Places so dark, so void of hope, that even the thought of climbing out felt impossible. It wasn't just sadness—it was despair. A weight that pressed on my chest, my spirit, and my mind all at once.

And yet, by the grace of God, I'm still here. And somehow, so is the light.

One such occasion was when I was on vacation with Mary on the beautiful island of Hawaii when we were both in our thirties. We were staying in an idyllic beachfront property as it was meant to be a blissful romantic break for just the two of us. We both desperately needed to get away just to relax together.

During this intended break, an idea happened to pop into my head one night about Pioneers and what they sacrificed for so many of us.

The dream came to me in such a prolific way that I immediately got up and woke Mary to tell her what had just happened. I told her that I felt that I needed to write a musical that would speak on this issue. I felt it should be a children's musical pageant that was based on the experiences of our pioneer ancestors who had made hazardous journeys by wagon across the plains of America in the 1800s to finally settle in the Salt Lake Valley. I could see it all so vividly that it stopped me from sleeping.

I wandered down to the beach alone for the following three days and nights. On my small handheld cassette player, I recorded everything that was flooding into my brain. I was so high on creative energy, there wasn't a tired bone in my body. Concerned, Mary would come out with food and drinks and to check on me.

At the end of the three days the whole project was finished. All the songs and the music were written, and I am glad to say that

CHAPTER NINE

the result of my manic, highly creative behavior in Hawaii still lives on today.

Over the years the Pioneer Pageants have given hundreds of children, all dressed in costumes from that era, the opportunity to sing, dance, and act out the Pioneer stories on stage.

In 2024 it was held in Cedar City with nearly 20,000 attending. My son Justin has now taken the lead for the event (The Pioneer Pageant) and I am so proud of him. He was able to secure many sponsors to cover the costs. The spectacular firework display was unbelievable. This event has grown each year and I am so pleased with the direction it is now heading in.

But, of course, the euphoria that I felt on completing the script in Hawaii didn't last. Not long afterwards I crashed. Mentally and physically, everything went black, and I couldn't stop sobbing uncontrollably.

Nothing made sense and I had to be hospitalized as doctors tried with different medications to balance the chemicals and lack of them that were causing the mayhem in my frazzled brain and get me back on track.

Another time was in the early seventies before I was married to Mary. Everything was going just great, record sales couldn't be better, our tours were selling out—outwardly, I had nothing in the world to worry about.

I had a loving family around me and my faith which always gave me the base when everything went wrong. But inwardly, as you probably know by now, it was a different story. On this occasion, I was driving the family car and I didn't want to live. Feeling low and tearful, I decided to head up to the top of the mountains and pray hard to see what could be done. But all I could see, or feel, was darkness.

In the glove box of the car, it was no surprise to find a Bowie hunting knife as we were outdoor people when we were not performing. As I sat there, I remember a windstorm so intense that it was almost scary. I had my window down and it almost blew me over. I felt so strongly at that moment that it had to be an intervention. I knew then that I needed to keep thinking straight, someone wanted me to live. Snapping back into reality, I put the knife down, but things could have turned out very differently that day had that timely miracle not occurred.

All in all, I have experienced four breakdowns of varying degrees at various decades of my life. One, I know, was sparked off by financial problems and another was just plain overload of work. Sometimes, it's not very clear what triggers me to suddenly go down that far.

In the past, nobody really talked about mental health, and I was left to deal with the highs and lows that came with my sensitive and creative mind alone.

Yes, some great work came out of it at times, but others were so bad that I truly did not want to live. During one spell where I needed to be hospitalized in my late twenties, I became so stressed, my blood pressure was rocketing so high that I suffered a mini stroke. I was told by doctors that my body was shutting down. If Mary hadn't realized that something was seriously amiss, hours earlier at home and raised the alarm, I guess I wouldn't be here today. I literally owe my life to her.

Thankfully, knowledge, treatment and good medication have now improved, and my condition is better managed though still not without careful monitoring. Nevertheless, close shaves and testing times happened for me and my family.

Not all the close shaves have been of my own making; there was the moment that I've already mentioned briefly when we as a family

CHAPTER NINE

learned from our attorneys that the Symbionese Liberation Army had put a death threat on our lives. After kidnapping the 19-year-old granddaughter of the American newspaper baron William Randolph Hearst, our, now famous, family had become a target.

As I wrote in my journal aged 20, 'We have just been told by the FBI that we've received a major death threat from the SLA regarding Patty Hearst's abduction. The whole family gathered to hear our options. They have demanded that certain Osmonds leave the entertainment business by a certain date, or we be killed. Patty was a fan I guess, and they got her diaries and are trying to destroy her thoughts and brainwash her.

Well, what an interesting situation we had to deal with. My brothers and I have been deputized and I just went to a shooting range to get certified to carry a weapon.'

But the Osmond family didn't quit the entertainment industry. We were all deputized and had security teams watching us individually.

Only when the whole drama ended with a police shootout in California, were we able to relax a little.

There have been three times when a threat to my life has popped up out of nowhere. Once was in Branson, Missouri, performing with the brothers at the time when the police caught up with a man in the audience who had a shotgun, a pistol and an axe in his possession. Apparently, they had acted on a tip off from his wife.

When I heard this, I had a real urge to meet this guy who wanted to harm me. The police refused at first saying he would just get into my head, but I was adamant that I wanted to meet him. I needed to know why he wanted to kill me.

Eventually it was agreed that I could visit him in his cell, where two officers were guarding him.

The whole time I was there, the man was sitting on a chair with his head firmly down. When I asked him, what in the world I had ever done that would make him to want to kill me, he remained silent. For the next half hour, I repeated that question time after time with no response.

Finally, I thought, 'Oh what the heck, let's get out of here.'

As I left the jail cell. I kept looking at him. Just then, this guy raised his head and gave me a smile so eerie it sent a chill down my spine. He did get into my head! That devilish look will be etched in my brain forever.

I wasn't alone in being a target and once even our father and baby son Travis were targets too. Mary and I were walking back to our hotel room where Father was rocking Travis close to the window. Through the trees in the grounds, I happened to spot a man dressed all in black holding a rifle pointed at them.

Totally panicked, I yelled: 'Hit the deck' to Father as the man dropped his rifle and calmly slipped out of the courtyard. By the time the police arrived, he was gone.

On another event in 1981, Governor Ronald Reagan had arrived earlier in Salt Lake City to wrap up his campaign to be the 40th President of the United States. He wanted to meet The Osmonds.

Excited but nervous, we agreed and were honored to hear that, should he win the election, he wanted us to help produce the Inauguration Ceremony in Washington D.C. He also wanted the Tabernacle Choir to sing the Battle Hymn of the Republic and wanted to know if we could help arrange that.

To make a very long story short, when he did win, I got in touch with the Inaugural Committee to check how we could get involved and we were invited to meet its members.

With Mary and my two assistants, Bill Critchfield, Bill Waite, and brother Alan by my side we made the trip, but it was soon made very clear to us that they didn't welcome our help.

CHAPTER NINE

Various people advised us to step back and forget the idea due to the level of bureaucracy involved. But being serious about this incredible opportunity and a bit stubborn, I didn't want to just pull out.

I could literally see in my mind how wonderful it would be having The Tabernacle Choir, a parade and fireworks—of course—involved in the show.

The problem was that not only would I be responsible for our part of the event itself, I also had to raise almost one million dollars to make things become a reality.

Given a deadline, I immediately got stuck into the fundraising business. But it soon became evident that we were not getting enough financial support to even make a dent in the amount we needed.

During this time, I also was suffering with massive depression and taking strong medication to keep my mind focused. Bless Mary, she stood by my side and gave me encouragement to keep me going.

The phone calls kept coming from my team saying that time was running out and that we either needed to plead for money or just call it quits.

Even a prominent church member, Williard Marriott, who had been the inaugural chairman for President Nixon, struggled when storms hit his event, canceling many elements of his program. Brother Marriott refused to help as he felt he had embarrassed The Tabernacle Choir and the church. I asked him for at least $50,000 but again he refused. All I remember was feeling completely depressed as I flew home. Was it all worth it?

Again, Mary kept me thinking straight. She knew the importance of this. I continued to try and raise the money. I basically lived in my recliner.

I found out something quite unique during that time. Those that had the money refused to give it but those that didn't have the money, gave it. It was a strange life lesson.

More pressure and more anxiety filled my mind. With my bipolar condition, the highs and the lows continued to hit me hard. Thank goodness for good medication and a strong wife.

I continued to hang in there and I also had a wonderful relationship with President Hinckley, who served in the first Presidency of our church. When I called him about having the Tabernacle Choir perform at the end and at the opening inaugural ceremonies, he told me the choir had already been contracted to go to Japan during that period but if he could get a direct invite from the inaugural committee inviting the choir, he would take that and see if he could reschedule their trip to Japan.

So now, my integrity was on the line. I told him that if I could not raise the funds in time, I would call him immediately. (I learned after everything was over that President Hinckley did reschedule the choir trip to Japan based on our conversation.)

But what made things even more intense was that I would have to raise the funds to get them back to the inaugural. The cost of two Boeing 747s, the housing costs and food was a staggering amount of money.

Three days before the deadline, I was sitting in my chair, praying with all that I had when my phone rang. It was Karl Lindner, the President of an American financial corporation out of Cincinnati. I don't know how he got my number, but he asked me if I was in charge of the opening Inaugural ceremonies, and of course, I said yes, I was.

He asked me what kind of money I was looking for and I told him I wasn't even close to the million dollars needed. He then said, if I could guarantee him a seat next to President Reagan, he would wire $750,000 that day. I flew out of my seat! I guaranteed him

CHAPTER NINE

his seat, of course, and he did wire the money to my personal bank account within an hour. Again, my integrity was on the line—based on my promise he had wired the money.

With the money I had in the bank, and now having Karl's money, it took me to where I needed to be. I immediately called President Hinckley and told him we were on! I called my team and told them, 'Arrange the aircraft!' as well as all the details surrounding their needs while in Washington DC.

I believed that I had just experienced another miracle. I've always believed that faith always preceded the miracle. I had been taught that by my mother earlier in life. I had witnessed that so many times when I sincerely believed in something that needed to be accomplished.

The other individual that helped out tremendously was the American philosopher and sociologist Ted Nelson pledging $50,000.

Overcome by a feeling of total euphoria, Mary and I got down on our knees and thanked our Heavenly Father for this miraculous moment.

A few calls later and everything and everyone was now on fire! Until a few days later when I received a call from President Gordon B. Hinckley.

He told me that he had received a letter from the inaugural committee uninviting The Tabernacle choir. He asked me what was going on. I don't think I have to describe what went through my mind and soul, only to say I almost died with shock and embarrassment.

Somehow, the words came out of my mouth: 'President, this will be resolved, don't worry.'

He calmly replied, 'Okay.' I now had to make sure they were re-invited. If I'd been unaware that certain people didn't like me or didn't want me involved in the inauguration before that call, I now had no doubt of it.

Steaming with anger, I got back on my knees and prayed fervently that I would have the strength and that help would be given to me.

I called the White House and pleaded to speak with the elected President, I was told that couldn't happen but I could leave a message with Nancy Reagan's assistant. I did as suggested, and it was a very emotional one. I made calls to everyone else I could imagine but never was able to get anyone's help.

The following morning, I got another phone call from President Hinckley telling me that he had received another fax re-inviting the choir. What a turnaround of events in just 24 hours!

Just before the big day, the opening event I'd carefully planned to involve The Tabernacle Choir, and the United States Army Band, singing 'America the Beautiful', 'Battle hymns of the Republic' and 'The Star-Spangled Banner' on the steps of The Lincoln Memorial was under threat again. Not only were storms raging, but a section of scaffolding that held a major firework set collapsed with one of the workers on top. It killed him.

The United States Secret Service, seeing what had happened, canceled the event. I immediately remembered what Willard Marriott had told me about his fiasco with President Nixon's inaugural. The same thing had started to happen to my event. Members of the choir became sick and needed to be taken to the hospital.

I went into a little trailer and poured my heart out to Heavenly Father. I asked for forgiveness for my actions; I had failed. Then within seconds, a knock on the door was heard. It was the Secret Service screaming out that the event was back on! They couldn't stop the President's escort from showing up.

Again, being completely shocked, I took a bullhorn and screamed out to all the technical people to plug everything back in. I was experiencing another miracle. Four of the firework companies were able to reconfigure their synced-up computer systems with each other

CHAPTER NINE

to execute the firework cues in a timely manner. Now that, alone, was the miracle. Technically that is quite impossible, but somehow it happened.

Nothing short of another miracle happened right after. Not only did the winds, hail and ice storms stop but the clouds in the sky parted enough that we could even see stars. My father, who knew all the details of what had happened from the beginning, grabbed me, and started to cry. Everything we had planned went off without a hitch.

The following day I was in charge of the float that would carry the 300 voice Tabernacle Choir to the exact spot where they could sing 'The Battle Hymn of the Republic' to President Reagan. This had been what he asked for in that little meeting in Salt Lake City. The float was built in two pieces; half was built in Washington DC, and the other half was built in our Utah studios.

The moment arrived. The float started down the street. When it was close to its mark, Bill Critchfield, one of my right arm guys came running up to me saying that the parks and recreation department said that under no circumstances would the float stop. If that was the case, the choir would not be able to sing their song to the President. It would go straight past him.

Going back to reading my journal entry, it wasn't completely clear if it was Bill Critchfield, Bill Waite or myself that pulled the $200 out of our pocket but we all agreed that if we could get the driver of the tractor pulling the float to 'flood' it, it would stop where it needed to.

We all looked at each other and said: 'Let's try.' The moment was surreal. On national television, the float stopped on the spot marked X and the choir sang the whole song to the President.

Those that watched the President during this moment remember the tears he shed. But, boy, we could have been in big trouble though. We actually paid the tractor driver off. Then I remember looking across the street at the viewing stand and seeing Willard Marriott applauding to the choir's song.

After the event, Mary and I were invited over to the White House for a little social gathering with the President and invited guests. President Reagan saw me, he waved me over into a little gathering which included the members of the inaugural committee that didn't like me.

President Reagan said, 'This has been the highlight for me. To have the choir sing The Battle Hymn of the Republic. That song was my desire from the beginning.'

Now, why I did what I did, I will never know, but I said, 'President, the credit goes to your inaugural team. They are the ones that made it happen.' I then backed out of the circle. Mary and I socialized a little before heading back to the hotel. I don't think I have ever felt so exhausted in my life.

After that I received a call in the middle of the night asking me to meet members of the Republican National Committee in the hotel lobby. I agreed and was asked if I would consider entering politics as my name had cropped up as one of several individuals who could be groomed for leadership.

Returning to Mary and recounting the conversation, her face said it all. It was blank! Politics was not to be my calling.

Back at home in Utah, recovering from the exhaustion, President Hinckley called with a problem. A pledge of $50,000 dollars to pay for the choir's expenses had fallen through. Chuckling at my shocked response, he went on to explain that Willard Marriott had already stumped up the money for the shortfall. Another miracle!

Thinking that was the end of things, I was then surprised to receive another call to say the seat for congress was coming up for the Republican candidate in Utah, where Robert Redford was considering running for the Democrat ticket. Would I consider running against him?

Days later, I received a call from Robert himself asking if I was considering running. I gulped and said I was. I had to say that. Well, I'm not sure if that was the reason he backed out, but he sure didn't run for Congress!

Chapter Ten

RUBBING SHOULDERS WITH IMPORTANT PEOPLE

※

One memory I'll never forget is when we were working on the family Christmas album. Our vocal arranger, Earl Brown, was known as one of the most creative and talented men in the industry.

He had high expectations for us, and we were determined to meet them. His challenging nature pushed us to study, practice, and rehearse until we had perfected the vocal charts he had given us.

Any musician studying the most complex musical strains would understand the intricate balance of melody, harmony, and rhythm that must be achieved in order to create a true masterpiece.

This was not an easy task for us. My brothers and I were not the greatest sight readers. The ability to sing unfamiliar music directly from a written score is a valuable skill for any musician. Our solution was to end up memorizing the various chord structures in our heads.

And to make it even more amazing, the orchestra arranger, Don Costa, took what we gave him on tape and constructed a masterpiece, adding who knows how many additional harmony parts to our already complex arrangement. At times, there would be seven to eight harmony parts flowing through a refrain or chorus.

Our newfound status in the entertainment world began connecting us with some of the biggest entertainers known at that time.

All at once, we were rubbing shoulders with some of the most amazing people—not just singers and musicians, but major actors, politicians, presidents of countries, and royalty.

I'll never forget the first time I met Frank Sinatra. It was at the MGM recording studio in Hollywood, California. The incredible Don Costa, the same Musical Director that would score our arrangements, was Sinatra's arranger too.

We were running late one day during our time in the studio. Don Costa looked at his watch and said 'Oh, oh, we need to stop right now. Frank Sinatra will be walking through the door any second and he demands full attention from me.'

Knowing who he was, we quickly ended our session and tried to get out of the studio. Everyone was extremely tense, especially the sound engineer, Ed Green. But before we knew it, Frank walked into the studio. We asked if there was another door we could escape by but there wasn't. Ed said, 'Just sit quietly and he probably won't see you.'

That truly was interesting; we learned two facts about Frank Sinatra in that setting. He doesn't allow people to see him record, and he would only do one take of a song. If someone in the orchestra made a mistake or even if he made a mistake, it's just too bad; he's walking out. To us this was just fascinating to watch.

Well, he did recognize us, as he saw us sitting there in the booth. He was a very kind gentleman, thank goodness. But what I truly can remember was how cool and calm Don Costa was in conducting the orchestra for a one-take song with Frank Sinatra standing there on a microphone.

CHAPTER TEN

The record button went on, the orchestra lit up, Frank Sinatra started to sing. And I didn't hear one mistake. He then said goodbye and walked out the door. That was it.

I'll also never forget the first time I met Elvis Presley—the King! Elvis had a residency at the International Hotel in Las Vegas. On top of that hotel, he had an enormous suite that took up the whole floor. He had a private elevator that took him directly to the stage.

During that same period in 1973, we, the Osmonds, had a three-week contract at Caesar's Palace, just down the street from the International. Our security at Caesar's Palace contacted Elvis's security and arranged for a meeting after both of our shows had ended.

During the 70s, we both had security issues that kept our protection teams jumping on a daily basis. We headed over to the International Hotel and were taken into a holding area while Elvis's security checked out our security to make sure everyone was legitimate. I remember it taking almost an hour for that to happen.

Finally, we were led into his dressing room and told to sit on a couch and wait for him to come out from the area where he got dressed for all of his shows. He finally opened that door and asked us to come into the room. He was dressed in a black robe with his name embroidered on it. I remember him pacing back and forth, talking to us about our two careers. He told us two things that I will never forget. He said that if he had to do it all over again, he would go out into the audience and shake everyone's hand. He truly missed that opportunity.

The other thing was that, when your fans start bringing their children to your shows, you will have then passed the generation gap. He also opened up a little closet and showed us all of his jumpsuits. He told us that we should dress in jumpsuits like his. He went on to say that a designer named Bill Belew should design them for us.

Another thing that made an impression on me was that he liked wearing different colored belts on his jumpsuits. The reason being, Elvis was truly into karate, and it represented the GI (Government Issue) karate belt as he called it. We must have talked for a good half hour with the King of Rock 'n' Roll. He asked us if we liked karate, and every one of us said yes. He then recommended that we contact a karate instructor named Chuck Norris.

That half hour with Elvis was—and still is—a memory that I will never forget, but this would actually be just one of many other encounters I had with him.

We ended up contacting Chuck Norris. At that time, we didn't realize how popular that man was, but he took our call. We told him that Elvis Presley had recommended we get in touch with him to see if we could start karate lessons.

So, we started lessons on a regular basis. When rehearsals at the studios or concerts ended, we would all end up at his studio. He was patient with us and worked with us on a private basis. He got us to the point where we became instructors in Tang Soo Do, a form of Korean karate. The self-confidence I gained in self-defense was truly awesome. I kept thinking of all the times in my earlier life when I felt I was going to get beaten up at school or have a hat pin shoved in my behind. I wonder what I would have done had I been an instructor during that time? The influence of karate could also be seen throughout our career. The West Side Story dancer, Jamie Rogers, who became our choreographer, took a karate style and used it to create new dance moves that made our stage routines truly unique.

One last remembrance I have of Chuck Norris was standing around him in a circle as he demonstrated a round kick. I guess he didn't see me because I was directly behind him. All I remember is that I was kicked in the head and saw stars for the rest of the session.

CHAPTER TEN

I'm not sure Chuck would even remember that, but that incident caused me to have a plate put in my neck, and L3, L4, L5, and S1 discs had to all be surgically replaced. I was now worth more inside my body than I was outside.

I also remember years later when the International Hotel contracted us to move over to the same hotel where Elvis performed. He was contracted for a three-week engagement. When he was done, the Osmonds moved in for their own three-week stint. That routine happened a few different times. One day, when Elvis was supposed to have moved out of his suite, we moved in. Mary and I had just been married, and the family gave us Elvis's bedroom.

I remember walking into that room. The curtains were black, the bed had black sheets, and there were no lights on except for a television playing. I squinted hard and eventually saw Elvis in bed! I remember he was wearing dark sunglasses. On seeing us, bless his heart, he said, 'Oh, I'm sorry; I'll get out of here soon.' I remember saying, 'Oh, please don't. Take as much time as you want, Elvis.' He got up, said hi to all of us, and then went down his private elevator.

I don't know if my brothers even know this, but Elvis was responsible for assisting me to develop a mental state that helped me perform better on stage. I used to watch him very closely while he performed. Even if he messed up the words to songs, he just laughed it off and went on. Having always tried to give a perfect performance on stage, when I messed up, not only did I take it hard, but I was always reminded that I did.

The last time I remember talking to him was at an event held in honor of Nancy Sinatra. Elvis was sitting there on a stool, and hardly anyone was around him. Something told me to walk up to him. I don't know why we started to talk about performing, but we did. He said something to me that I believe was meant to be said, and it truly changed the way I thought from that point on about singing on stage.

His exact words, based on my journal entry, were, 'Stop trying to think about every word you're singing. Stop worrying about the dance steps too. Change the mode of your thought process by putting yourself into a daze; switch on the automatic pilot inside your head.' He said he did that every show.

That advice has helped me more than anyone could imagine throughout my career. Being trained to be a perfectionist, I could never relax on stage, worrying I'd mess up.

One last thing that I will never forget was how close he was to my mother. It was like our mother was his second mom. On so many occasions, my mother would talk to him over the phone for hours. It truly did blow me away. But that's my mother; she was not fearful of anyone. They were so close that Elvis and she talked about religion a lot. He truly wanted to know what happens after death. He loved the concept of the three degrees of glory, and those who chose to be close to the Lord and showed it would be rewarded not only in this life but in the life to come.

I don't know if many know this, but Elvis truly wanted to be a preacher. One of the important lessons that I also learned in mixing with other huge stars was to never, ever judge them by their public persona. When we got to know them off stage, they were very down-to-earth people. Most of the time, images are created by PR departments, managers, agents, and record companies that depict them as worldly characters. Why that happens, I really don't have an answer for, other than making more money for those who had invested huge amounts to create sensational imagery.

Perhaps one of the best examples of that was our encounter with one of my favorite bands of all time, Led Zeppelin. One day, we were booked to play Earls Court, one of the biggest venues in England. It was in 1975, and Led Zeppelin was going to follow us the following day. Because of the screams from the fans at our concerts, we could

CHAPTER TEN

never push the decibels over the screams. We needed the loudest sound system we could find, and Led Zeppelin's was the only system that could do that.

It just so happened that the Zeppelin system had been put in on the day of our show. Our manager reached out to their manager and asked if we could possibly use their system for our show and he was nice enough to allow that to happen.

After Zeppelin had finished their show, our manager got word that the band would love to meet us. Now, the image put in our minds was that they were going to be a drug-fueled rock band, a world away from our own clean-cut image.

We all headed backstage where they had just performed. What a surprise I got when I found their children running around and their families all surrounding them. This changed my entire outlook. They were some of the nicest guys I had ever met. Now, for sure, their audience was very different, and there was plenty of marijuana drifting around, but the band members themselves had more in common with the Osmonds than perhaps we had given them credit for.

Other encounters I've had with other successful entertainers also gave me a lot of hope. For three years, between 1976 and 1979, my brother Alan and I were the executive producers of the Donny & Marie Show. It aired every Friday night on the American ABC channel.

During that time, we played host to some pretty amazing guests, including Andy Williams himself. Having Andy Williams on that show, who had given the Osmonds our big break, truly was humbling, to say the least.

Raymond Burr, who played the iconic lawyer Perry Mason, who also had a popular TV show, the $6 Million Dollar Man with Lee Majors, and his Charlie's Angels wife Farrah Fawcett, as well as the singing duo Sonny and Cher. Every week, there would be bigger and bigger names showing up.

One guest singer that I'll never forget, though, is Raquel Welch. Not for the reasons you might imagine. Upon arrival at the studio in Utah, she announced that she wanted to wear a dress by the designer Bob Mackie.

As he was one of the most famous and expensive dress designers of all time, I knew there was no way we could afford it. I told the network that, but because this lady was so popular and could probably bring more ratings to the show, they agreed to pay the extra money for the dress. So, we built a huge set reflecting the same color dress she would wear and put all of the dancers in the same color.

When it was time to tape her portion of the show, her manager walked out on stage and started to talk to our stage manager. The next thing I heard was, 'Osmond to the floor.' That was my cue to run down and see what the problem might be.

Raquel Welch's manager said she didn't like the dress. Shut down everything until she finds something she wants to wear. Now, to give you an idea of how much money was being spent: camera crews, lighting, stage managers, dancers, and so on were running up costs of $2,000 a minute.

I began to chuckle. I said, 'You're joking, right?' That manager looked me in the face like I was a child and said, 'No one's kidding.' Now, being only 25 years old, I guess you could say I *was* a child, but I was also the executive producer of the Donny & Marie Show and felt the pressure of at least the network executives who were in the booth.

I'll never forget this. Four or five executives began to chat. About 15 seconds later, they looked at me and asked, 'What would you do if you had to make the decision?' Being extremely upset, I said, 'If it were up to me, I would fire her.' They all then said, 'Then go do it.'

CHAPTER TEN

I believe that's when my hair started to turn white. I went down on stage, told the stage manager to go get Raquel's manager, and to meet me on stage. He came out. I looked him in the eye and told him that if she did not come out on stage within fifteen minutes dressed in her expensive dress, I would have a car waiting for her outside to take her to the airport. I also said that she needed to leave her dress in the dressing room.

I've never seen a man's face get so red as he ran off. For fifteen minutes, everyone held their breath. Well, hallelujah, she did come on and did her big number. I usually say goodbye to everyone upon their leaving our studio, but this one time I didn't. That was one of the big stresses I had to deal with during that period of time.

Well, that wasn't over yet. The family had built a nice apartment building that we called the Star Quarters. This was a location where all the stars came to the show to stay. We had our own police force that would be positioned there night and day. We also provided a personal chef.

Raquel Welch was one of the guests staying there that night. And in one of the other condos connected to her guest room was an actor and comedian named Buddy Hackett. In America, he was a fairly popular comedian as well.

Well, in the middle of the night, I received a phone call from our security telling us that Buddy Hackett, who had been drinking, had broken into Raquel's apartment. I got in the car and met the police at the apartment. Raquel Welch, being as mad as she was, obviously didn't help the situation. We had to physically pull Buddy back into his room and put locks on the door.

I went back to bed. I was then woken up for the second time a couple of hours later. An alarm had gone off. Buddy had broken into Raquel's apartment again. This time, we had to physically take him off-site and check him into the Marriott Hotel. We put three guards at his door throughout the night.

Thank goodness the show that we had just taped had been completed. So, we hurried and arranged transportation to take them both to the airport.

Another time I got a call from Robert Redford. He kindly let me know that Buddy Hackett was up at his ski resort—Sundance—buying up a storm, tons of ski equipment, gear and merchandise, all being charged to the studio's account. Bob and I had a friendly arrangement, we helped entertain each other's guests from time to time—so this heads up was appreciated.

The thing was Buddy was supposed to be at our rehearsals, he hadn't shown up and now I knew why. I jumped in my car and headed straight up the canyon to see what was going on. Sure enough, there was Buddy, completely drunk and having a grand old time and refusing to stop buying.

It wasn't easy but I managed to talk him into coming back with me. I told him, 'Buddy, I'll make sure you get out of here before this gets out of hand.' Somehow he agreed. It was one of those wild unforgettable book of showbiz friendships.

As showbusiness disasters go, they don't get any worse though than tripping up Nancy Sinatra on stage on her opening night. Nancy worked with us on a dance routine for weeks prior to her opening night. We were confident that things would go well.

Everyone you could imagine was in the audience that night. I mean, just to mention a few: Frank Sinatra, Elvis Presley, Tom Jones, Sammy Davis Jr., Dean Martin, Neil Diamond, and half the entertainment industry were there.

You could tell that Nancy was very stressed out. Knowing that her dad, Frank Sinatra, was sitting very close to the stage made her uneasy.

CHAPTER TEN

As the band started to play the opening number, she stood in the middle of the brothers as we began to go out on stage. The choreography was not very complicated, but somehow Nancy put her foot in front of Alan's, tripped, and fell to the ground. We hurried and tried to pick her up, but she pulled away from us. We did not know what to do, and neither did the band. Finally, the band stopped, we walked off stage, and there she sat crying.

After a period of time, Nancy regained her composure because in true showbusiness fashion, the show must go on. Thank goodness she knew that. We all knew that we would be fired. Because we were still on the show, we went out and did our 15 minutes, then headed back to our dressing room.

After the show had completed, no one came to our door to say anything. Everything just remained quiet. We surely didn't want to go out of the room and say anything to Nancy; we had no idea what she would say to us. Then suddenly, someone knocked at the door. Two guys in suits and hats stood there. They said that Frank Sinatra would like to speak to us.

I'm serious; there couldn't have been more stress and anguish possible. He walked in with his big blue eyes and asked if he could sit down. He said that he appreciated the professionalism that we had shown. He felt bad Nancy had fallen but it wasn't our fault. The way he handled the conversation with us was something I will remember for many years.

The day we met Julie Andrews on the stage of The Andy Williams show, I became her biggest fan. She was not only one of the nicest ladies I had ever met but she was willing to take the time to teach us the song 'Supercalifragilisticexpialidocious'—we also learned to sing it backwards, which I can still do today and have taught my grandkids!

Cher was another individual that I have come to know as a true friend. When we performed with her on TV, it was one of those experiences where we bonded immediately. Her work ethic and her professionalism to get things done correctly was very impressive to me.

I remember a time when we were in rehearsal with her, she sat down to take a breather. I was also out of breath and walked over to her and sat down with her. We had a nice little visit. I'll never forget asking her how she was able to keep up with her busy schedule. She was ready to go on tour the following day after taping this show. She looked at me with a smile and said, 'We just keep going, don't we?' She truly was a hard worker and one of my heroes.

But one moment that I will never forget was one of the biggest mistakes that could have ever been made. One of the stupidest moves that any young producer could make was this:

Fairly often during that TV show, there would be moments when people wanted to audition. It was very difficult to try to put someone new on the Donny & Marie Show because it was network-driven, but it was neat to be able to meet good talent and possibly give them some advice.

On one occasion, this little gal from Canada came onto the stage and sang like a bird. She had the most beautiful voice. At that time, we had no real connections with the record industry per se, and we were contracted to do television shows for the next few years. We told her that we would keep her name in mind, but there was nothing we could do at that moment.

Guess who she was? None other than Céline Dion!

If I'm completely honest, of all the celebrities that I ever crossed paths with, I think I would have to say that meeting Elvis Presley, Paul McCartney, John Wayne, and Her Majesty, the Queen of England, were probably among my highlights.

CHAPTER TEN

I've already told you about the first time that I met the Queen, but I am honored to say that I met her on another three separate occasions as well.

Those experiences have provided me with some fascinating memories. There was always a strict protocol in place when meeting her.

The whole thing made me pretty uptight. But clearly, our mother had more nerve. On the occasion in question, our mother broke all protocol and handed her a copy of the Book of Mormon, saying that it was the most precious thing she could give her, and the security staff looked anything but happy. Yet the Queen was extremely gracious and thanked our mother for presenting that to her. While everything seemed to be going just fine as she continued to move down the line, as she reached me, I just happened to be licking my lips, which had gone dry because I was going through one of those nervous spells.

After a little conversation, she moved on as photographers snapped away. Although I was aware of all the photographers being there, I was shocked to see the following morning's newspapers carrying my picture on the front page with the headline: 'Osmond Sticks Tongue Out at Queen.'

Those camera guys captured the very moment that I had been licking my lips. It's highly unlikely that I will ever forget it, but just in case I do, that photograph hangs on my office wall and still makes me sick. I'm not sure why I constantly want to be sick, but who in the heck would ever do such a thing but me? I was probably the most hated man that day when the newspaper published that picture.

The next time I met the Queen, I was worried that she might remember me as being disrespectful back then. But I didn't have to worry.

Once again, she moved down the line and eventually came to me, only to ask, 'Merrill, how are you today?' Then she chuckled. Now, she might have been well-briefed by her advisors, but I was truly honored and relieved that she not only chuckled but that she knew my name. There are so many stories from that time that it would take probably 100 books to get through half of them.

The day I met Howard Hughes—one of the richest and most influential men in the world—was an interesting one. We were playing the Riviera Hotel in Las Vegas. The Riviera was a location where it was rumored that Howard Hughes would stay at. Historically, when we were performing in a location, nobody was allowed backstage, except for those who assisted us with clothes or make up needs. But this night was different.

Right before the end of the show, I noticed off stage that a line of people had entered the backstage. It seemed very odd to me. As we took our final bow and ran off stage there he was, in a wheelchair, with five or six guys standing by his side. He wanted to meet us. It was interesting to me that those that stood next to him were members of our church. They worked for him as his protection team.

Lucille Ball was a lady of perfection. She demanded perfection in everything she ever did throughout the show. She worked with brother Donny the most, and I remember her being very tough on him, getting him to become stronger in dialogue and be more in character as he was acting in the show. We went to her home on occasions and were able to just get to know her better then. Again, one of the individuals that made a difference in my life.

One of the days I will never forget is when Bob Hope and I became good friends. I was producing a major stadium show in Nashville, Tennessee. I hired Bob to be the main star of that evening's attraction. I had co-written a song called 'The Hope of America' with my friend Cliff Maag. We wrote it in honor of Bob.

CHAPTER TEN

When the time came for Bob to record the song in a recording studio, he had already seen the lyrics and music beforehand so he could be ready for the studio session. When the moment came, where he put on his headphone and stood up to the microphone, he stopped and asked where I was. When I heard him ask for me, I ran out and stood next to him.

He asked me to sing the song to him so he could get it into his head. I did that a few times as he sang along with me. Now, this is what I will never forget—he really wasn't getting it very well. A few takes were made, but he was not on pitch or in time. He again asked me to sing it to him. Then a thought came into my mind. I asked him if he would feel better if he took one of the headsets off on one ear and let me sing it a half a second before he sings the song. Now, anyone who has experience standing in front of a microphone, listening to the track, keeping your pitch in control and keep it entertaining, knows how difficult this would be. But he thought it would be a good idea. When the track started, I was able to sing a half a second of the song in his ear before the downbeat he was required to sing. He recorded it in one take. Now, that was a professional!

It's taking me some time to try to put even this book together, but it's just the tip of the iceberg. Many of the stories I've forgotten until someone or something might jog my memory.

Another memory that I have laughed about for years was in the 70s with Mary's 'spit wad' attacks on me while I was on stage.

She would hide behind my 8ft Marshall amps on stage, take her straw, put a little rolled up piece of paper in it and shoot that at me. She would aim to hit me in the head and neck throughout the show. I always knew she was there and it actually wasn't very funny back then, but we both laugh about it now as we remember those fun moments.

There are so many journal entries that take up at least 50 book binders that I get frustrated trying to take the time to go through it all. Maybe when I pass away, my kids will take the time to read just how bizarre it was for their old dad to experience what happened to him.

When I met Barry Manilow on his big final tour in New York earlier in 2024, he reminded me of the time when he'd astounded my sister Marie by popping out of a box at the Hilton Hotel to surprise her with a little puppy. Marie was 13 years old at the time and was overjoyed to receive this cute little puppy, which was called Mandy after his big hit.

Another memory I have is of Kenny Rogers. My brothers and I were doing a TV special one year and Kenny was one of the guests. During a break we sat down and had a good talk. I remember Kenny seemed really discouraged and he was in the process of leaving The First Edition and told me he was ready to quit the music industry. I was sitting across from him when he said, 'I'm done.'

Being a lead singer myself, I've always admired his voice. I told him he had one of the most unique voices I had heard and it would be a real loss if the world didn't get to hear it. I don't know if my words meant much to him but I gave him my two cents. The rest, as they say, is history.

I'll never play down how exciting and unforgettable it all was back in those days, but so many new life issues started to create unbelievable troubles for us. And there were some pretty significant ones. If I wasn't a member of the Church of Jesus Christ of Latter-day Saints, there's another, stronger word I would use.

Chapter Eleven

SQUANDERING MONEY IS WRONG

Nothing had ever come easily to our father. Everything he owned had come from sheer hard work and being prudent with money.

By comparison to his childhood, our early lives were blessed thanks to his and our mother's efforts. We didn't know how it felt to go hungry or to worry about having a roof over our heads. Living on a farm in Ogden, we grew our own organic vegetables and our milk for cheese and butter was on tap from Daisy the cow.

Our mother was an excellent cook who believed in feeding us good wholesome food. She was quite ahead of her time really by making sure that our diet was organic where possible and supplemented with nuts and vitamins where necessary.

Remembering only too well how poverty felt from his own childhood experiences, our father was keen to make sure that we had a sound attitude to money from an early age.

As much as our Friday night family dinners were about coming together, good food and entertainment, he also would instigate financial discussions.

Not a believer in handing out pocket money for us just to squander, he thought that we should plan how we would spend any money before we received it.

Each week, we all had an opportunity to make a bid for money for, say, a new bike or camping equipment. Then, over dinner, the whole family would discuss the proposal that was on the table and decide whether it should be approved.

As well as teaching us about finance, it also taught us negotiation skills, something that would come in useful years down the line when negotiating recording and TV contracts.

If we couldn't come to a firm decision, the request was put to a family vote which Father always had the right to veto.

We even had a family investment project where we took out a mortgage to buy our first shared property. Each week, we would have a progress report to see how the mortgage loan was reducing.

It was a lesson that stuck. An indication of this can be seen by my journal entry, aged 20: 'I took my sweetie to dinner and spent all our money. No, I take it back. We have a buck and a half left. And it's only the third of February. So, we better tighten our belts.'

Romance was one thing, but reality wasn't far from my thoughts thanks to Father's lessons.

'None of my boys has grown up up to be a fool with money,' he was proud to boast to people.

Imagine then just how excruciatingly painful it was for the Osmonds to lose all the millions that we'd spent our lives building up. After all those years of hard work.

At the peak of our success, the Osmonds were worth millions. Most of it went into a central family fund and invested. Even when we were married, Mary and I were only given a small monthly allowance to exist on.

CHAPTER ELEVEN

After things changed for the Osmonds when the enormous success of the Donny & Marie Show turned out to be at the brothers' expense, it really hit home financially. With the record companies pulling out, there wasn't even any money available for demos. So, we just shut down.

We were in the show but more as a variety act. But we were dealing with the network, and the ratings showed that certain things sent the ratings up like the sketches we did at the start and the end of the show.

People were either saying 'I cannot believe I am watching this' or they loved it.

We saw a pattern building. If we weren't making the ratings we wouldn't be getting any money so it was controversial some of the stuff we were doing. Wayne wanted out so badly.

With hindsight, perhaps we should have listened to Wayne more. He was the one who wrote Crazy Horses really; it was his guitar licks that did it. Wayne is my hero, he had absolutely no guile, no ego but I knew where his mind was. He just wanted to rock like Led Zeppelin and, sadly, he never got the opportunity. It's too late now but I just hope he gets it in another life.

The good news was that by then we had got into the television industry.

We got behind the Donny & Marie Show, and I am proud of my siblings for that. The ego did not come up. It would be hard given that dressing up was often required to take part in the show. You can't go on stage dressed in a lobster outfit, as Wayne was, or a bookcase, as Jimmy was, and be self-important!

We could have bolted but instead we got behind the show and got stuck in, producing and directing. It was really cool. I became a television producer and then president of Osmond Enterprises.

But it was a rough time mainly because I would have to hire and fire people and, with my personality, it was not a good day for me if

I had to fire someone. You know what I used to do? I used to have Mary bake cookies and bring them into the office and put them on my desk.

Whenever I had to fire someone, I had them come in and gave them a cookie. I kept them there and cried with them!

As time went on, I was becoming more and more stressed doing what I was doing. I had been put in charge of things for a couple of reasons.

One was because we were starting to understand there were problems going on with embezzlement.

I was only 28 years old but the family wanted me in there to find out what was going on so I hired all these account agents, ex Internal Revenue Service people and we tried to find it. But try as we might, we just couldn't find it.

It was about that time that we decided to move the making of the Donny & Marie Show to Utah. Ever the visionary, it was our mother's idea.

She said, 'If you can make it in California doing what you are doing, let's go to Utah and build a studio.'

And so, we got together as a family like we always did and we all voted. The one who really didn't want it was Wayne. Wayne just didn't want the studio built but the rest of us voted 'yes' so we built the studio.

Again, we should have been listening to Wayne. Maybe he was bothered about the money. We put in a lot of money, millions. We had our own union, we had our own police department. We had cop cars everywhere. We bought aircraft to fly people back from California. We literally created an industry and a whole lotta jobs in Utah during those years.

But then came the problems. When the Donny & Marie Show wasn't recommissioned in 1979 for another series, it was a major

CHAPTER ELEVEN

loss. As I have said, showbusiness is fickle and trends change. We just didn't see it coming. With our studios out in Utah, it was also often difficult to get technical staff and performers out there afterwards.

As I was basically running things for the Osmond entertainment company, we would still go out on the road and perform, and then I would come back and sit in the office and hire or give out cookies.

But one time, we came home and found out that our homes were mortgaged; the studios itself, that had been debt-free, was mortgaged to the tune of millions of dollars. Every single asset we had was mortgaged and we did not know anything about it.

What we did next—and, again with hindsight, it was a big mistake—all of us voted to let someone into our partnership. Well, we let this individual, who ran the Osmond entertainment industry, have a ten per cent stake and he was the root of our troubles.

And that is when I, on behalf of the family, brought in six Arthur Andersen agents—that was the big financial firm back then in the United States—and they could not find the trail.

The trail went everywhere so the family lost, I think it was $80 million.

We had invested our whole lives in that so when the studios went down, well... And here's the other thing, the man running it started doing X-rated movie distribution in the basement of the studios. When we found that out our mother went whoosh! Oh boy, you don't want to get our mother involved in anything like that.

So, we had to get rid of him but, you know what, he took all the software, he took the productions and he'd taken all the money. We were left with a studio full of debt and that's all. Everything was mortgaged. The man is now passed.

I was raised to believe people when they said they would do something and I've learned the hard way that you just cannot always trust people. As much as I want to trust people, there are times when my heart gets broken.

Like Michael Jackson, we too have complained about how record companies can rip an artist off. Having sold over 100 million records, you'd think that the Osmonds would receive quite a bit of money. But a dishonest record company will hide the real profits made if they can.

In our case, in the 70s we sent an accountant to do an audit on our royalties. He had an interesting name for an accountant, Lou Costly. We should have engaged an entertainment accountant to do the work, but Lou was a good old boy our father had used for years.

When Lou went through the audit with a man by the name of Dick Rising(another interesting name), they came away with enough money to get our attention, but it wasn't even close to what we should have earned. When Lou got home, one night he received a phone call from Dick Rising and said, 'off the record' you need to look under a certain file number. He said you might be really shocked at the numbers you'll find. Numbers that were hidden from your original audit.

Lou told us what he had been told. Lou then arranged another meeting with the accountants at the record label and he asked to have Mr Rising in the meeting. Lou was told that Dick Rising had died a couple days earlier. We found out later that he mysteriously died in his bathtub. But the autopsy showed he died from natural causes.

Lou never did find that certain file Mr Rising had told him to look for.

I've lost more money on a handshake than I think anybody has lost. But as much as Jays musical wants to blame me and Alan, we all jointly made the decisions that cost us dearly. As I have already explained, it was always the Osmond way.

CHAPTER ELEVEN

Do you know something? It would have been less painful and more profitable for us just to go bankrupt but being such a man of honor, our father simply would not allow that.

He refused to leave other people with unpaid debts because of their dealings with his family. So, we did what we have always done when we've needed money: we got back up on stage at his insistence.

Another world tour beckoned, and we paid back every last cent of our debt doing the one thing we all knew how to do: perform.

Since then I have made and lost even more money. Around 15 years after the family financial crisis, I experienced another one. This time it involved my own personal finances. Mistakenly but acting in good faith, I had loaned too much money over the years to friends without receiving adequate security for repayment.

It created so many problems. Creditors would no longer work with me and there was no-one in the family I could turn to for financial support.

It all came at a price to me and my own immediate family and my marriage. Poor Mary had already lived through one major financial loss.

Naturally, the worry and shame of it all affected my health – both physical and mental. This was around one of the times that I had to be hospitalized. But, once back on my shaky feet, I set about earning again for the sake of my family.

Reflecting on my life, as I've been writing this book, money and the lack of it, has sent me down some strange paths throughout my life. We were raised up with money. We had quite a bit of success in that area. But I hope that we will always be remembered for our rock n' roll stuff.

Mary and I even uprooted our family from Utah to move to Branson for five years to perform with my brothers at a theater there.

It had been Jimmy's idea to do so in 1992 and we worked extremely hard six days a week. It wasn't easy.

What you might find strange is that all the Osmonds will say this: if we had not lost all the money, none of us would ever be performing still. We would have gone off and done something else.

But, having lost everything twice, I can honestly say that I am grateful that I did.

Life is not about money; it's about the experiences that we go through when we have heartaches and what we learn from them.

When all the Osmond family money disappeared, our mother just calmly repeated her old saying: 'Oh well, this too shall pass.' And it did.

A very young Merrill

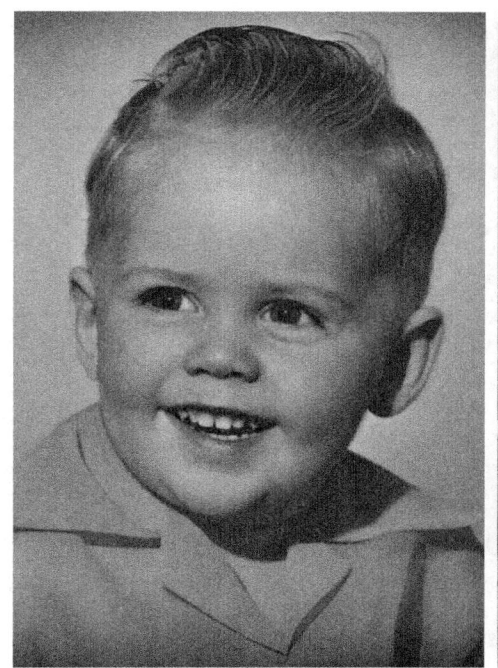

The young Osmond brothers

The Osmond family, 1965

On the Andy Williams TV show

Singing with Julie Andrews

With the Williams brothers

The Osmonds' horn section

Merrill Osmond
14 h

Another picture I'd love to keep for my Grandkids to see, sadly all these gold records were stolen.

With Bob Hope

With Mother and Father

In 1971 (clockwise from lower left: Alan, Wayne, Merrill, Jay, Donny)

With The Carpenters

With George Burns

With The Bee Gees

With Ronald Reagan

Father and Mother

Mother working on our farm

This is how I remember my father

The Osmond family making music at home, 1960s

With Mary and the children in the 1980s

My last photo taken with brother Wayne, March 2023

With my youngest, Sheila

My son Justin and his family

My daughter Heather and family

My son Travis and his family

My son Shane and his family

2015 performing with Susan Boyle (Photo credit Dustin P Smith)

The Merrill Osmond family, April 2022

On Family Feud, 2024

My buddy, Barry Manilow, invited me to his show in 2024

Having fun on stage with my guitarist Phil Hendriks

Promo photos by Dustin P Smith

My 'brick in the wall' at The Cavern

Receiving an honorary doctorate from Dixie State University, 2017

Promo photo by Dustin P Smith

One of my final shows, 2024

Donny Osmond ✓
36 m

It was a night I'll never forget. I went to my brother, Merrill's final performance here in the US. As I watched him perform some of our greatest hits, I was actually transformed into a fan myself as I sang along with all of the other fans that packed the Westgate theater, formerly known as the Las Vegas Hilton where we used to perform as a band back in the 70's. Merrill asked me to join him at the end of the show and as he sang his closing song, I couldn't help but give my brother a big farewell hug.
Yes, it took all of us to create the band called The Osmonds, but it was Merrill's voice that created the sound of The Osmonds.
It was an amazing moment.
Thank you, my brother.

Donny's Facebook post after my final US show, 2022

Chapter Twelve

HEROES AND A SAINT

Coming, as I do, from a family that has an amazing ability to not only perform with the best, but also to remain true to their strong convictions, I've got to say that each single member is a hero to me. One is even a saint…

I have never known a man that had more humility than my brother Wayne. He was a man with absolutely no guile; an individual who was quick to forgive and had the ability to show unconditional love to everyone he ever met. Those men are truly rare today.

Wayne was a saint before he came into this world, and he has left it as an even greater saint.

When I learned that my dear brother had suffered a massive stroke, my natural response was to immediately fall to my knees and pray for him to receive the assurance that his mission had been accomplished, and he was successful in this endeavor in many ways.

Afterwards, I set off to drive to the hospital in Salt Lake City to see him and say my goodbyes. During that long drive I was filled with so many emotions. I was able to spend some time with him alone and I am so grateful I was able to have those last moments with him.

The following day Mary and I were working in the Temple when we were told the news of Wayne's passing.

His departure from this earth will be a sad moment for some but for those who are waiting for him on the other side, there will be a massive celebration beyond anything we can imagine.

My brother Wayne was the first Osmond brother to pass and he endured much. He gave it his all. His legacy will go down as someone who was not only a genius in his ability to write music but was able to capture the hearts of millions of people and bring them closer to God.

He and his sweetheart, Kathy, had just celebrated their 50th wedding anniversary a month earlier. The funeral was January 11th in Ogden, Utah. The family requested it was attended by family and friends only, but it was so heartwarming to see all the wonderful tributes to Wayne on all the TV networks—he was loved. Wayne never liked funerals and told his kids when it was his time, he wanted a party not a funeral!

Something happened after the funeral I would like to share. As the hearse and cars were driving to the graveside down the freeway, someone was having a party and had released some balloons into the air. They were heading towards the freeway and came down in front of Wayne's hearse. The car drove into them but instead of popping, they became tangled on the back bumper so the hearse was traveling down the freeway with balloons blowing around on the back of the bumper. When the car pulled into the graveside, they all suddenly released themselves into the air. I guess Wayne had a party after all!

I will miss him tremendously. I am so grateful to have grown up with one of Heavenly Father's greatest sons.

On a lighter note, in this chapter, I also want to talk about two of my siblings who have professionally surpassed all of us in enduring the test of time. Not that any other sibling hasn't done their fair share of work over the last six decades... But Donny and Marie have

CHAPTER TWELVE

proven that they were able to reinvent themselves throughout the years. That is something that can sometimes be virtually impossible to do in an industry as fickle as the entertainment industry.

I will start by paying heartfelt tribute to my sister Marie. I know that people have problems. I know that people deal with disastrous issues that could take them down. I understand how losing a loved one can cause depression so severe that the thought of not wanting to live can cross one's mind. Having been born into our family, I also know how the word 'perfection' can create unbelievable torment when a mistake occurs. All of this and more has been the case for my little sister, and I wish to pay tribute to her.

Marie was raised just like the rest of us, but our parents were a little bit easier on her. She was called our little princess, and that's the name we still call her today. No one but her siblings know the extent of the pain and suffering that she has experienced throughout her life. Those who have read some of her own books know about some of this, but as her brother, I feel I can share some things with you that you might not be aware of.

To begin with, she understood what stress was about at a very young age. When her brothers were hitting the charts with number one records, she and our mother worked tirelessly with the fan club, making sure that those who wrote in either got an answer or even a phone call if a life-disastrous moment could possibly occur. The true nature of my sister was that she was a loving, caring, and extremely humble little girl.

One thing Marie never had that the rest of us brothers did… was a sister to talk to. Someone who could understand her from that same place. We had each other to lean on, but she carried so much alone, without that kind of sisterly bond to help her through it. I've often thought about that. It must've been very lonely for Marie at times—not having that kind of connection. Thank goodness she had a loving mother by her side. That bond meant everything, especially in a world that could feel so isolating.

When the idea of having her sing 'Paper Roses' at the age of 12 came up, I watched very carefully as the producers of the song worked with her. Giving it all she had was very stressful for her. Having watched her brothers record and feeling the same mental challenge of being perfect, she had to grow up fast. There was really no time for her to be a little girl, to go outside and play with friends. She was now in the limelight, and those who surrounded the Osmond family had their eye on her.

Having a hit record with 'Paper Roses,' the record company immediately went crazy, making sure that an album would come out quickly. Being the middle brother, and with a sensitive heart, I watched how she dealt with all of that pressure with a smile on her face. She never complained. As I have been writing this book, this chapter probably means the most to me. After years of seeing her record her music or seeing her on stage playing with her band, I am always amazed at how she was able to do it. I know she's always had nervous conditions like I have, but for some reason, she was able to hold it together a lot better than I did.

When the Donny & Marie Show was created, we siblings worked day and night trying to help produce the shows. We literally stopped recording and went into the television business. Here is what most people will never understand:

It's one thing to create an hour-long program with comedy sketches, opening and closing productions, major choreography, and songs that needed to be recorded with perfection. Dealing with major entertainers who had their own personal issues, like ego and pride, and doing all of this in one week for three years in a row raises the question: how in the heck was that even possible?

CHAPTER TWELVE

But take all of that and then add the fact that everything needed to be memorized within a three- or four-day period. The complicated choreography alone baffled me, and I was used to learning choreography at quite a fast pace, but this was something else! No way could I accomplish that. Then consider all of the songs for the opening and closing segments. Not only did they have to learn a skating routine on ice, but they had to do it with perfection. Most times, they would only have to do it in one take. I'm sure the other siblings would agree with me that that alone would be impossible for us.

Then there were all of the sketches. Obviously, there were cue cards for their lines, but as an executive producer and someone on the floor watching the sketches being performed, I rarely saw them look at the cue cards. They were able to memorize their lines, and once again, usually doing it in one take. For me, at least, I would've had a nervous breakdown.

Then would come the impossible for me. During the 'Little Bit Country, Little Bit Rock 'n' Roll' segments, rehearsing could only take two days because there was so much to learn in other areas of the show.

After all the rehearsals during the day, they would go into the recording studio and record their pre-recorded vocals, and then the next day they would not only lip-sync with perfection, but all of the choreography staged by my brother Jay would be in perfect step as well.

I looked at my journal the other day while I was writing this and literally said, 'I truly believe my brother and sister are aliens.' I honestly had tears in my eyes at times.

Then I'll never forget the day we found out that each show had gone way over budget, and everyone involved in the show didn't know what to do. I learned later that the individual who embezzled money from us had used part of the budget money to invest in other projects, and none of us knew that.

So, knowing the dilemma, the decision was made to tape three shows a week. Did you read that correctly? Yes, three shows in one week. All I can say is major miracles happened. What I personally saw during that week still haunts me today. I still get weak just thinking about it.

Her life has been well documented throughout newspapers, tabloid magazines, interviews, and deceptive paparazzi who always tried to get a scoop that would create a stain on her reputation.

What I know, and will keep silent about, is the hell she went through during her marriages. Regardless of what happened with Steve, I always felt that he was the one for her throughout all eternity, despite a few problems. That Cinderella story did come true, and the two of them are totally in love and have learned so much that their bond will last forever.

Her second marriage, which no one in the family wants to talk about, was a disaster. What you all probably read in those same tabloid magazines is true. That relationship physically and mentally drained her.

I don't feel it's my place, even though I know many details should be shared in my book. I know she has written about some of her life stories, but the one story about losing her little son, Michael, not only broke her heart but also caused a lot of mental damage. How my sister has been able to deal with and conquer all that has been thrown at her over the years is absolutely unbelievable.

Now, I'll close with these thoughts about Marie. Those of you who have read many of her articles or her books know that she is a very deep thinker and is very wise. My sister and I believe in the 'no accident' theory. There are reasons why everything happens. I know my sister well enough to tell everyone to just watch her. If you think you know her next move, you are incorrect. She takes her direction

CHAPTER TWELVE

from her Heavenly Father. She has a relationship with Him that very few people have.

I don't know Marie's destiny, but I can tell you that she is not finished with her work on this earth. She is just like my mother: very visionary, very spiritual, very intellectual, and extremely humble. All of those qualities qualify her to receive divine direction. Marie and I are very close, and she knows I love her to bits.

Now to my next hero. For most of my siblings, our physical ability to do much more in the entertainment industry has pretty much ended. We have all felt that our journey and our mission here on earth has been completed. Even though you'll hear occasional posts and see a few events produced by certain siblings, the chance of seeing us all together again on one stage won't happen. And if I'm wrong, you all have the right to throw tomatoes at me!

Brother Donny has also been my hero. Back in the day, when our first records started to happen, I was known as the lead singer. However, when Donny became so visible and well-known as a major teenage idol, that lead singer position sort of faded for me.

A lot of people have made comments over the years saying I was jealous, but I would laugh about that. You see, what people don't know about our family is that it's always been 'all for one and one for all.' If an ego crept into our family at a young age, it was crushed. It was stopped. It was destroyed, and thank goodness for that. Our father, having been a military sergeant, understood very well how to handle that issue.

If you all remember the early days, you'll recall that brother Jay was the one out front, sitting on the steps of the Andy Williams show. Not one of the siblings ever even had a thought about Jay taking the limelight; we were just grateful that all we had worked for over the years was being accepted by the public.

Ever since Donny stole the show when he first joined us with Andy Williams, as a young boy, our motto was 'It doesn't matter who's out front as long as it's an Osmond.' The thing I always admired about my brother Donny is how he handled everything that came at him. I'm sure that his own books have probably given some of you an idea how he has dealt with his unbelievable issues throughout the years.

Donny has always possessed an extraordinary ability: the gift to envision something, process it deeply, and then bring it to life—almost as if he were shaping matter with his mind and spirit.

To craft a solo career after growing up within a family identity is no small task. It requires courage, patience, and vision. Donny has shown a steady hand in the storm, a willingness to take the hits, to learn from them, and to keep moving forward with a sense of higher purpose. He has learned how to discern the right path to walk—balancing the demands of the world with his own internal compass.

But what many may not realize is that Donny also had to navigate the emotional weight of rising popularity—not just in public, but within his own family. That kind of spotlight can stir up ego and pride, and it can be hard for others to understand or accept. But Donny handled it with grace. He didn't let it divide him from his roots. He stayed grounded, respectful, and wise beyond his years in how he carried that responsibility.

And when you reflect on the role he played as Joseph in Egypt, it's hard not to see the parallels. Joseph was chosen, favored, misunderstood, and yet rose to a position where he could preserve and bless his family. In many ways, Donny has walked a similar path. Whether he knew it or not, that role became more than just a performance—it mirrored something deeper, something almost destined.

That takes strength. And I've seen it in him time and time again.

CHAPTER TWELVE

'D,' as Marie and I call him, dealt with issues that could have destroyed their union over the years, but it didn't. I witnessed people trying to get in the middle of their relationship, trying to be the big guy presenting ideas that could separate them for personal gain. But just watch us. If there ever were issues that created tension among the family, we would always work them out. We have been through a lot of issues that took time to resolve, but it always did get resolved in the end.

D has been nothing but supportive of my solo career in my later days. He has always been there for me.

It seems Donny is carrying the torch at this time for the family but keeping an eye on Marie.

He knows his mission and he has a belief system that by staying true to what he knows is right and being a good example to the world, the rewards—not only here on this earth but also on the other side—would be worth every negative issue that has ever gotten in his way.

You see, no one is perfect. I surely had to learn that myself, having made so many mistakes in my life. But I finally came to the realization that if you do not make mistakes, you'll never learn from them. D has had good people surrounding him and a loving family of his own. Sound advice is what he has received. I could write so much more about my brother, but suffice it to say, he has earned the title of hero in my life. And I don't have very many of those titles to give out.

Chapter Thirteen

BLACK BEAR

※

From the very start of our relationship, Mary has always understood the affection we received from female fans. Mary saw it firsthand when she was helping my mother and Marie sift through the millions of fan letters that the Osmonds received every week through the fan club. Mary has had to endure more than most people will ever know—dealing with over obsessed fans who, at times, would stop at nothing to tear her down or pull me away from her. There were moments when I honestly wondered why she didn't just throw her hands in the air and walk away. It was that bad. But she never did, because at the heart of it all Mary and I shared a bond that was eternal rooted in our love for each other, our family and our sacred commitment to God. That's what kept us together, that's what held us firm.

One time, a freight company delivered a huge box. When it was opened, it contained two girls inside it. Almost unbelievably, our fans had mailed themselves to us! Now, that was a first, even by Osmond fans' standards. On our wedding day, thousands of tearful girls lined the temple gates, hoping to catch one last glimpse.

Mostly, it was innocent—the innocent emotion of teenagers with crushes on me and my brothers. And honestly, without that passion, we wouldn't have sold so many records or filled so many venues. We loved our fans, even though the sheer number of them could feel overwhelming in crowd situations for me when younger.

But years later, the adoration turned darker. What began as admiration eventually twisted into something far more dangerous: obsession. Today, stalking is a well known threat, but back then, it was rarely talked about and often dismissed.

I've already shared how I came to be known as Bear in my family. Black Bear evolved as a protective code word—something we began using around 2009, especially in hotels and venues. It became a kind of lifeline, a signal for safety.

For me, 'Black Bear' isn't just a name. It symbolizes both strength and the shadows I've endured—childhood abuse, breakdowns, depression, anxiety but especially strength.

The kind the Native American tradition attributes to the Black Bear. The kind I have needed to survive.

Our first serious experience of stalking involved someone who was eventually convicted and served prison time. She had moved to our hometown, attended our church and loitered near to our house. We had to get court orders to protect our family.

But another woman followed and this one never stopped. To this day, we still have to deal with her. She had done everything she can to insert herself into our lives—even though everyone knows my heart truly belongs to Mary.

It was while facing this ongoing threat that we fully activated the Black Bear protocol—more than ever before.

One of the hardest things for me, as the object of one female warped desire, has been witnessing the devastation it has had on the lives of the people closest to me—Mary and my kids, of course, but also those working close to me on a professional level. This includes my Personal Assistant, Tracey Beaumont, who has suffered repeatedly from this person since she started working for me in 2009.

Tracey entered our lives at a time when I had very little left in the tank. My solo career had stalled, my confidence was depleted and the stalking was escalating. She already knew my son Justin, through charity events, and quickly became an essential part of the team, especially in her work with The Hearing Fund in the UK. More importantly she became someone we could trust. She didn't judge. She just helped and her loyalty would be tested again and again.

She set a few things in motion that really helped me get back on stage to launch a new solo career. Tracey is still working with me and my family in a way that no one else ever has. Tracey and her husband, Dave, are two of my closest allies today.

Journal Entry—November 2008
Mary and I found out our email accounts had been hacked. Passwords changed. Total control lost. It's hard to describe the fear of knowing someone is pretending to be you—writing to friends and business contacts in your voice. I feel completely exposed. Mary hasn't been sleeping.

Life with me has never been easy for Mary, I don't think the words exist to do justice to the trauma this fan obsession has put Mary through over the years. Although it is widely accepted that many women fall in love with stars they see on stage and screen, and it's usually harmless, this was taken to another level entirely.

One of the things I have noticed about the stalkers who have followed me is that they begin to identify with you on a personal level. They think they are with you; they believe that you and they are a couple and simply ignore all the family and friends you have around, treating them as if they are of no consequence. They truly believe they are a part of your personal life.

After one particularly troubling incident—involving someone who became known to the family and who was treated kindly by all of us—Mary has admitted that it nearly caused her to have a breakdown.

'This person put me through hell, and I have never regretted something so much in my life,' Mary told family members and close friends, some of whom witnessed the problem with their own eyes.

'She would do literally anything she could to get to Merrill. She acted like a friend of the family, always offering to help, but all she wanted was Merrill. There were so many nights when I cried myself to sleep, not knowing what she would do next. I cannot begin to tell you how much stress and worry she created for my little family.

'On tours where she was helping, she would set up something for me and the kids to do so she could be alone with Merrill. It was obvious pretty soon she had become obsessed with my husband.

'I saw it; our kids saw it; our friends saw it, and even fans were talking about it. We would all constantly tell Merrill of things that she had done and said.

'As Merrill and I read back on my journals, written at that time, it brings the horror of it all back to me, and it seems difficult to understand how we let someone like that so readily into our lives, but it was done slowly, over time, on the pretense of helping us all the time.'

This is still painful for us to talk about but it shows what this particular stalker tried to accomplish. The disturbing depth she was willing to go to in order to manipulate, deceive and insert herself into the most sacred and private parts of our lives. This wasn't a case of casual obsession—it was calculated, relentless and spiritually destructive. She didn't just want access, she wanted control. She made it her mission to dismantle everything good in my life, especially the sacred bond between my wife and me.

She would play on sympathy, twisted truths and even used others as pawns in her pursuit of something that was never hers to begin with. But what she couldn't understand was this: we were protected by something she never had—true love, a deep faith in God and a family bound together by a purpose and prayer.

Her actions were not only disturbing, they were dangerous and yet through it all my wife never wavered. She stood firm even when everything inside her must have screamed to run. That, to me, is the definition of strength.

The trouble is that from the very early days of the Osmonds, there has always been a huge entourage around us, and it is relatively easy for people to abuse their positions should they have a mind to. Most don't, of course.

One time a leather company had stepped forward to sponsor me and I was given good quality black leather stage jackets and pants in return for advertising their clothing. It was a good deal, and I signed it with a promise Mary would be able to go and choose herself a leather jacket also.

On the day we went into the store to choose her jacket, the staff on duty just looked embarrassed and we had no idea why. They had to explain that someone who said they were working for us, had already been and claimed the allowance set aside for Mary's jacket.

Journal Entry
Someone walked into a leather store, claimed to work for me and took the jacket Mary was supposed to receive. The staff were embarrassed when we turned up. Mary just looked down and didn't say much. It felt like a theft of more than just leather—it was a theft of dignity.

Looking back to those days, I now feel that we were too trusting—almost naïve, maybe—but we always liked to see the best in everyone and couldn't imagine that people could behave in such ways.

When we had experienced the behavior of overzealous fans over the years, we had grown to half-expect it, but some of the things that happened to us were on a completely different level.

Around the end of 2008, we found out she had hacked into our private email accounts. All the passwords had been changed, and so they had complete control of everything. This was a frightening time for Mary and me as in 2008 it wasn't as easy as it is today to resolve issues like this. Internet hacking and social media security wasn't as secure as it is today. I certainly wasn't as computer literate back then as I am today.

I was hearing from friends and family who had received emails that I had supposedly sent to them! It was obvious to those who knew me that these weren't from me. Some of them were just shocking, others were in response to work offers, but this person was answering as me, in my name. Again, this was putting so much stress on both Mary and me. Remember, this was 2008, before phone and the internet had the preventions that are in place today, and we just didn't know what we were dealing with. It simply wasn't recognized back then.

Journal Entry—December 2008
We are hearing from friends about strange messages they are receiving from me. Offers accepted, requests denied, things I never wrote. This woman—who once offered help—is clearly behind it. I feel sick. Mary is crying almost nightly. We are now using the name Black Bear more frequently for security and family code.

CHAPTER THIRTEEN

It's a horrible, intrusive feeling knowing someone is reading every private piece of information that you send or receive, as this person clearly was. The thought that someone was reading all our deeply personal correspondence to our friends and family was just too much for all of us. We would change passwords and start new email accounts and we were very careful who we gave these to. We didn't know until later that an iCloud account had been set up in my name at an earlier time and all our accounts were then automatically linked to it, allowing this person to have all our new information.

Today, this would be dealt with very differently and thank goodness it's recognized in ways it wasn't back in 2008.

Throughout all of this, I was still having to go on stage and perform, knowing that the person responsible could be in the audience. I needed to keep on working, and in some ways, it was an escape from what was happening, but there was always an underlying worry. The thought of someone emailing family and friends or replying to potential job offers as me, in my name, was frightening.

We were all afraid of what could happen next. Maybe this person would try to blackmail us or go to the press to tell highly personal stories about the family. After all, she had been welcomed by us with her offers of help.

It was a ridiculous situation when I couldn't get onto my own social media accounts, such as Facebook or Twitter, but someone else could. Anything could, and sometimes was, posted in my name. We were always raised to protect the family name and I knew the press would have a field day if they found out. Looking back, I think that's the reason we didn't act sooner.

Journal Entry—January 2009
We still can't get into some of my social media accounts. Someone out there is posting as me—saying things I would never say. Promoting fake shows and selling fake merchandise. We're scared the media will pick it up. It's humiliating. Our lawyer is involved but it's slow going.

This person had photos, copies of contracts, and journals belonging to us at one time, and it took us years to eventually obtain them back through our lawyer. These had been held in safe keeping when 'helping us.'

There was also the matter of many of my merchandise items which to this day we never retrieved. We later found out the same person still had some of my journals and was refusing to return them unless I called her and personally asked. I wasn't prepared to do that after all the trauma she had created for my wife and I, and was about to go legal with it. Our good friend Steve Brick was the person who helped us retrieve these items. He called and warned her that we were about to go to the police. They were returned to us within days.

We were so grateful to him because it was obvious the person involved had somehow convinced herself she was in the right and for some reason known only to herself she thought she owned a part of us. Desperate people do desperate things.

Steve remains a good friend of ours today. I would like to mention Steve here as he has demonstrated not only loyalty but defines the truest friend possible. He helped both Mary and myself when we were dealing with this person. I was introduced to him through Donny, many years ago, and as a family we appreciate him.

We even had my official website, http://www.merrillosmond.com/, hacked into. That is the domain I own, but there have been

CHAPTER THIRTEEN

instances where very similar-sounding domains popped up online, and it is always without my permission. One site claimed to be my official website and started directing fans to it and even selling 'signed' goods in my name! It was in direct conflict with my own official website and was an unauthorized representation. Naturally, we feared it could affect future event bookings, especially when images and information had been copied directly from our official site without our permission. This person clearly had no knowledge of copyright laws.

What was more annoying was that the fake site's address had previously been owned by The Osmonds, but ownership had expired as it was no longer used by any of us and was only retained for this purpose. The domain hadn't been re-registered as ours. Someone already knew that and had taken ownership of it themselves.

I spoke with Jimmy about my concerns, and he immediately said we needed to contact our lawyer, Jason Turner, who said it would take a few days but he would have it shut down, and thankfully he did. Jimmy saw what we were going through and how it was affecting us, I will always be grateful for how he helped us during this time.

All this comes at the price of being famous. Not only are you a target for people trying to rip you off, but you still must deal with obsession. This became a continuous worry and caused both Mary and me enormous stress. Little did we know, this person would continue for years after.

Journal Entry—June 2017
She showed up in St George. Posted photos from our street.
Ate at one of our favorite restaurants.
That restaurant? We've never returned.

One time this same person drove over 1,500 miles just to visit our little town, St George. It was a deeply unnerving experience. I was away in Chicago working on a consultancy project at the time but that wasn't public knowledge. We soon realized this person would assume I was in St George too.

I was at a medical conference I was contracted to attend twice a year in Chicago as a spokesperson but we never posted about it and there were no details on any of my schedules or online dates so no one would know this. It was a deal I had outside of the entertainment industry with a company called Medical Billing, and I had represented them privately for many years.

Mary was at home with our youngest son, Troy, and she received a phone call to say a photo had been posted of our street and the same person was then eating lunch in 'Merrill's favorite local restaurant' and was going 'bear hunting.' Why on earth had she driven for at least two days to come to our hometown? Normally we wouldn't be worried about this but after the recent events Mary called me fearing the worst. I told Troy to close all the windows, lock all the doors, and I ordered both to stay at home, which they did; Mary had been planning to go out later, but I asked her to stay home. What a horrible way to have to live. That was one of our favorite eating places but to this day we have never returned since.

It still makes you feel uncomfortable, though, knowing someone who had already caused us problems was now prowling around your own street, your hometown, your sanctuary. You are supposed to feel safe there. People have tried the most ingenious ways to get close to me.

Journal Entry—January 2009
Mary opened up to someone she thought was from our PR firm, 'Faith Turner' she said her name was. Turns out it was all a lie. A fake email, using a real staff member's name. The

CHAPTER THIRTEEN

betrayal is crushing. We are getting legal advice again. But it feels like we are still one step behind.

Another time, Mary received an email from the public relations (PR) firm we always used, saying they had a lady in the office called Faith Turner who was able to help us with our administration work until we were able to get a new assistant.

We had no reason to doubt this, as we had used this same PR firm for many years. Again, in hindsight, we should have been wiser. In fact, it wasn't the public relations firm emailing us at all, but the same person emailing us directly! She had opened a fake email address using their name to make us think it was them. She even used the same name of a lady who did actually work there in the office to make it more convincing! Obviously, she had obtained every scrap of knowledge she could about our professional and personal lives.

It was our daughter, Sheila, who had reason to call 'Faith' one day, and was suspicious, she contacted us immediately to warn us. Mary called the PR company direct, and they said they had no idea we had been approached, and they also sought legal advice as they had then been falsely represented.

More worryingly, Mary had bared her soul to this 'Faith Turner', telling her in emails some of the issues we were going through and the effect it was having on her. Mary wasn't sleeping and we would receive calls during the night, but when Mary answered, no one was there. As well as revealing to her what was happening, she had told her what needed to be done and what we needed moving forward. Yet, all the time she'd been unknowingly playing into the hands of this person. It completely shocked us, it was all starting to become very scary. The lengths to which she was going to to gain access to me were escalating all the time. It was now clear to everyone. We spoke to our lawyers but I was also conscious of the Osmond name being leaked in the press. I didn't want a public lawsuit unless absolutely necessary. Our friends and those close to us knew the situation and were becoming increasingly concerned for us.

As I have already said, today this would be dealt with very differently and there were many, many more incidents involving this individual that I won't go into, but it created enormous stress for Mary and myself. The damage done to Mary during this time is hard to put into words. She tried to protect me and our family while holding on to her natural kindness. But that kindness was used against her. We thought it couldn't get any worse then she showed up in Branson.

Mary adds, 'Not long after that, we were doing a Fan Get Together in Branson. This was a paid event for fans, and it was fully booked. Somehow, this same person turned up unannounced, never paid, and sat herself down!

'As the room was full of fans from around the world and filmed by many, it was decided not to cause a scene in front of them. I was so mad that she thought it was okay to turn up like that after everything she had done and was continuing to do. We decided to change things so that all events we did were strictly ticketed and non-transferable after that.'

> *Journal Entry—October 2010*
> *She showed up at our fan gathering in Branson. Univited, unashamed, and unpaid. I wanted to have her immediately removed but the room was full of fans and cameras everywhere. We know now—everything has to change.*

Even the Osmonds' 50th anniversary celebrations in Las Vegas in 2007 could not escape her obsessive behavior. The family had been invited to perform with The Mormon Tabernacle Choir in Salt Lake City, and it was an honor for us all.

CHAPTER THIRTEEN

'A dream come true,' is how Jimmy describes the occasion. 'We've been overwhelmed with the response. This is the crown jewel in our 50th tour. We're thrilled to be coming home,' he said.

The choir and orchestra were also excited about the concert. Choir president Mac Christensen said, 'To share this moment with the Osmonds is unbelievable. To think of the example, they have set for the church and for the world—and yet they've always been ours, our favorites. We are really blessed.'

'We're delighted,' added Mack Wilberg, director of the choir. 'The Osmonds belong to the world, but they've always had a special connection to those in this area. Tonight, we will all be doing the things that we do well.'

All nine Osmond siblings were there, and it was meant to be an enormously joyous occasion, but then Mary got warned by security that there was someone trying to meet me backstage, and could she please confirm it was okay as the person wasn't on the security guest list. It was the same person we had been having problems with.

Mary told me, 'She was sitting there coolly eating a sandwich, even though she had no right whatsoever to be in the area or even the building. There was absolutely no reason for her to be backstage because she had nothing at all to do with the program and certainly hadn't been invited by us but she had somehow wangled her way in.'

Our security personnel immediately told her to leave, but Mary was really annoyed that she had turned up without being invited in the first place, and even more so that she had caused such a security issue backstage at such a special and sacred event for the family.

This was a performance watched by millions around the world, not just the Mormon church. The Tabernacle event meant so much to me and my brothers. I would like to say that stalking has finally come to an end for me, but alas, even today, I can't say that.

Journal Entry—2007
Mary was warned by security before our performance, someone was backstage and wanting to see me. It was her again. Sitting there eating like it was no big deal.

In February 2009 I performed at Busch Gardens in Tampa with my brothers. We were doing three shows a day over four days. This was always a fun week and had become an annual event. Fans flew into Florida from around the world and enjoyed the three daily outdoor shows in the beautiful sunshine. Everyone involved with the shows was aware of the situation and was looking out for her in the crowds. I wasn't overly concerned she would appear as I honestly didn't think she would dare show up again. How wrong I was!

I remember Jimmy saying he had scanned the crowds and said she wasn't there, so we were relieved, but as the first show started, I had just opened up the first number, looking out into the audience when I thought I saw her.

I wasn't wrong, although this time she was in disguise with a long blonde wig and dark glasses. I had to continue the show knowing she was out in the audience but then immediately informed our security people backstage.

Journal Entry—February 2009—Busch Gardens
I opened the show and scanned the crowd. My heart sank. I saw her. Disguised—wig, sunglasses but it was her. I had to keep singing. What choice did I have? Told security immediately. She had no fear. No Shame. I am angry now. She shouldn't be here, not after everything.

CHAPTER THIRTEEN

I couldn't believe she had turned up after everything and in disguise! I was angry that my family had to be constantly on high alert in this way. We would receive phone calls during the night and when we answered them, we were met with silence at the other end of the line. This would continue until we had no choice but to change our number again.

Tracey thought that she could deal with the situation herself at first, so she wouldn't tell me about some of the things that were also happening to her personally because she thought we didn't need the additional stress.

She had seen the effect it was having on Mary especially. It came with the job unfortunately. There was a lot to do around that time, as many exciting offers were coming in, including long solo tours at a level I had never done before.

It got serious when Tracey was awoken at 3am by a call from an American mutual friend of ours who had received an email from 'Tracey' but knew it wasn't from her because of the content. An email account had been opened in Tracey's name. The addresses were very similar apart from one digit so was very convincing. Only the most eagle-eyed internet users would know the difference, and this person then used the account to send damaging emails to Osmond family members and friends in Tracey's name. Again, this was in 2009 when not many of us were internet savvy.

The emails were very convincing, so much so that my son Justin initially believed them. He didn't know Tracey well enough at that time, and why would he suspect anything when it had her name on it? It was my daughter, Heather, and Tracey's husband, Dave, who were able to trace the IP address to prove who it was.

Justin feels bad to this day about this and still apologizes for not realizing that it wasn't Tracey. Happily, the two have a great relationship today and have worked together on many projects since then, but it could have turned out very differently.

Journal Entry—March 2009
Someone is using Tracey's name and sending lies to my family by email. Justin believed it at first. Can't blame him, it looked real. Heather and Dave tracked the IP. The same person. This is going too far.

Another worrying time was when our Twitter account was hacked into using an old device she had used when helping us years earlier and the device was still linked to the Twitter account unbeknown to us. We would notice certain curse words appear on our posts or photos would be altered and some of my posts were reworded, making me look very bad indeed and very unprofessional. An announcement would be posted saying a show would be canceled. It really was relentless during that time.

All of us would wake up each morning dreading what we would see. We changed passwords, but somehow, she was still able to access our accounts. It was worrying, as we couldn't understand how she still had access. We had to contact Twitter who explained the account was linked to another device. Until that device was removed from our account, she would still have access, even if we changed passwords. Today, thankfully, internet security is much better, and this would never get this far, but at the time it was very difficult to prove.

It became a highly draining process contacting social media websites like Twitter and Facebook and pleading with them to get something sorted. We were spending a lot of time trying to prove who I was, and we really were the people who were supposed to oversee the accounts. I'm just so glad that behavior like this is now taken seriously and help is readily at hand. Today, social media accounts are verified and much easier to control and safeguard.

We had to pay for extra security for the website when we set up a new one in 2014 to stop someone from hacking into it. The lady

CHAPTER THIRTEEN

who did our website told us she couldn't do it anymore, as this issue scared her so much. She had never encountered anything like this. We started a new one with an internet company that tightened our security, and no one was able to hack into the new one. It was a huge relief.

Journal Entry—September 2014
We've launched a new website—this time with tight security. The woman who built it before has backed out. She said the situation scared her too much.

But while it lasted, it was very upsetting for everyone. Tracey revealed that she had dealt with a lot more than we were aware of, and she confided a lot in Troy at the time because she didn't want to cause any more stress for Mary or myself. She and Troy became great friends and talked a lot about the problems it was creating.

Troy saw it for himself and had told me of his concerns when in September 2017 we held an event in Nevada. A relatively new direction for us in the USA, it was a healing program called Serenity devised for people to enjoy therapeutic treatments combined with live music provided by me. The idea was for people to go away feeling rejuvenated. We had done these in England, but this was the first one in the USA.

It was all a very unsettling, frightening time; Troy could see what was happening and all the posts on social media trying to damage our event, and he was angry that it was still going on in 2017 and the effect it was having on his family and those around them. We had been told by the venue that someone had tried to cancel the event just a few days earlier. But it was all the fake profiles appearing on social media discrediting my work and those around me that was most distressing. Tracey never responded publicly to the hurtful and derogatory posts about her, she never fueled the fire. She just kept loyally working.

Troy came to me to discuss things, and we decided that the best way would be for me to go public and post a video making it clear in no uncertain terms that it had to stop or further action would be taken. I didn't mention names. I hadn't done this before but enough was enough now. This was like a breath of fresh air! It all stopped immediately; posts were deleted, and there were no more threatening texts. Faithful fans began contacting us and apologizing for believing all they had read.

Journal Entry—October 2017
The video worked. Everything went quiet. Posts were deleted. It's a relief but a fragile one. We know better than to believe it is over.

The event went wonderfully well, and we could finally put this behind us, or so we thought. Alas, it was incredibly naïve to think this was the end of it, though. Posts and comments towards Tracey started to appear on social media, discrediting her ability to work for me and trying to undermine her or taking credit for work we were doing, even claiming to be working for me which obviously was untrue.

What this woman wanted most, we later learned, was Tracey's job. She wanted access to me. To Mary. To our life. When she couldn't get it she did everything in her power to tear it apart. It became relentless at one point and always became worse when I was in England or just prior to a tour starting, and we soon learned to expect something during these times. Over the years, staff from venues that had been booked would call Tracey to ask why she was canceling events. She used to have to tell every new venue to please double-check everything with her personally, as there was someone

CHAPTER THIRTEEN

falsely acting on our behalf. Again, this is where Black Bear came in as a code word to be used.

Tracey even received a deeply unsettling package, a book through the mail (personally signed by this same person) which had white feathers inserted between pages and certain words highlighted in pink. Mary and I were in England at this time and we were alarmed. I took it and destroyed it.

Journal Entry—June 2009
Tracey received a book in the mail. Signed. White feathers between the pages. The intent was clear. It's psychological warfare now.

We began to use the code name Black Bear at each new event to be used in all correspondence, but it was still a constant worry, as some of our events were high-profile black-tie Galas with up to 700 people attending, including many celebrities and VIPs. These were stressful enough to organize without the added concern of worrying what was going to happen next.

Journal Entry
Tracey said something that stuck with me today. 'Maybe if I had responded back then, we wouldn't still be dealing with this.' But I know she was protecting us, especially Mary. She's never fought back or responded publicly. Just stayed loyal. Steadfast. Strong. She's family.

Chapter Fourteen

CELEBRITY SURVIVAL

If I have any addiction, it's to nothing more dangerous than music. So many others in the public eye aren't so lucky, but sadly, that's rock 'n' roll for you. It's a tale as old as time. You only have to think of hugely talented stars such as Michael Jackson, Whitney Houston, Amy Winehouse, and George Michael, who've all fought and lost battles with substance or alcohol abuse and are no longer with us.

While I'm very grateful for the incredible life I've led and the amazing opportunities that fame as an Osmond brother has brought me, it's been a tough road to tread at times, and I've stumbled. My own four breakdowns at various stages of my life are almost as well documented as my achievements on stage. I just didn't resort to fighting them with illegal drugs, tobacco, or alcohol.

Food has been an issue, and I suffered from bulimia until I was prescribed the drug Lamotrigine at the age of 18, which is known to have an effect on unregulated emotions and impulse control.

It can't have helped that, as a young boy, I would stick my fingers down my throat and be sick to keep my weight down so I would look like my brothers on stage. At other times, Father would restrict my eating, and I would only get half a hamburger, unlike my brothers.

Somewhere, I guess, it created the idea in my mind that food was bad for me, while on the other hand, I couldn't control my appetite for it.

I have never taken non-prescription drugs, and other than one slip when I was sixteen years old, I haven't touched a drop of alcohol. The slip wasn't even intentional. It happened on a baking hot day in the early years when we were playing at an outdoor fair. Buckets of sweat were pouring off us all, and my father ordered us all a soda to drink. Taking my glass, I chugged it down in a single gulp, only to discover it tasted terrible. As we later discovered, it wasn't soda at all but gin! The waiter had made a mistake. Boy, what a shock.

What I've found out over the years is that those individuals who have received great stardom in their lives are usually the most precious, wholesome, and humble people you'll ever want to meet. Mainly because they've been through it, they know what it's like to experience ups and downs in their careers and personal lives. They always truly appreciate their fans.

I've never met more down-to-earth people than Kris Kristofferson and Rita Coolidge. I got to know them very well when they had both been invited to be on a brothers' special. It was a concert segment featuring just the three of us; my brothers had other guest stars that they'd been asked to perform with. Kris and Rita were two tremendously talented performers who were married for six years.

Individually or together, they were always great. In 1977, country legend Kris was the bare-chested man smooching with Barbra Streisand in A Star is Born. Rita, the original Delta Lady from the song, was one of the most in-demand rock vocalists in Los Angeles. As a duo, they won two Grammy Awards for Best Country Performance by a Duo or Group with Vocal in 1974 and 1976.

When the time came for us to begin recording them for the show, hundreds of people poured into the studio. The band was well-rehearsed, and as soon as we started, a kind of magic took over and ignited the whole room.

The director was so excited at the end of the recording that he wanted to repeat it two or three more times. Each time we did, the excitement escalated. When it was all over, I had a chance to sit down with them both and thank them for making my segment of the show so remarkable.

Kris invited me and my brothers to their shared home afterward, where we got the chance to know them even better. What we didn't see, though, was any sign of their 'volatile' relationship that Rita later opened up about in her own autobiography, where she talks about the problems caused by Kris's drinking and infidelity. It's a familiar story.

The Osmonds had always been fans of the British group, the Bee Gees, who were hugely successful in the sixties and seventies yet critically underrated. We'd performed many of their songs on stage. The youngest of the four Gibb brothers, Andy, was a guest on the Donny & Marie Show and sang a duet with Marie. The two of them dated for a time, but it didn't end well, and Marie had to take legal action to stop him from calling her. Sadly, Andy died aged 30 of heart failure.

I got to know Barry Gibb, who was the anchor of the group, quite well, and we quickly bonded. Having been in the business longer than us, he was always happy to pass on the benefit of his own incredible experiences, readily providing helpful insights into the recording industry.

As well as being a talented performer, Maurice was a skilled songwriter and arranger, and we called him to our Utah studios to help us produce an album. Sadly, Maurice truly suffered from addiction issues that caused him to make poor choices, and it was no different when he was in Utah.

Presumably out of shame and embarrassment, he tried to keep his demons a secret. But during recording sessions, alcohol bottles were hidden away everywhere inside the studios, even behind toilet seats.

Prone to making rash decisions when under the influence of alcohol, Maurice decided that he wanted to buy a cabin up in the mountains. When he saw my house in Provo, he figured that was the 'cabin' he wanted.

I couldn't understand because our large family home truly was not a cabin and nor was it in the mountains. He wanted it badly, though, and he also wanted to buy everything in it—beds, sheets, towels, pictures on the walls. Mary went ballistic at first but then relented when he made us a generous offer for everything.

When things hadn't gone very well one day, he decided on another whim that he wanted to leave Utah and go to Florida, no reason but he wanted to go there and then. I tried to arrange a flight for him, but it was past midnight, and no airlines were flying there. Maurice didn't want to take no for an answer. He continued to insist that he wanted to get out of Utah and get out fast, but it was impossible.

In desperation, he then asked me to hire him a private jet, but again, at that hour, everything was closed down, and there was nothing I could find to solve the problem.

Still not giving in, he said, 'I'll buy a jet if they can fly it in tonight.'

Now that kind of behavior really blew my mind, but I just blinked, looked through my list of contacts, and managed to find the owner of Falcon Jets. I called this man, waking him up, and told him what I was calling about.

'If you can deliver a jet into Provo, Utah, early in the morning, he will buy the plane.' Six million dollars later, and Maurice Gibb owned the Falcon 20, which arrived at Provo airport with a pilot willing to fly him to Florida.

CHAPTER FOURTEEN

We needed to finish the album we were working on, so I boarded the jet with him. So far, so good until we were around 25,000 to 30,000 feet in the air when suddenly Maurice pulled out a gun. As he screamed and yelled at his wife, who had been visiting us with him, the gun was pointing at her head. Oh boy, did this get my attention. I hurried to the cockpit and told the captain to start descending as quickly as he could. On hearing an explanation of the situation, he agreed.

One of our studio guys, Bud, was traveling with us, and we decided to jump Maurice together to try and get the gun out of his hand before he fired it.

Had he done so, Maurice would have caused the plane to decompress and crash. We felt that it was imperative to do it. I counted off, and we both lunged forward. Maurice fell down and knocked himself out.

On landing in Florida, Maurice's parents were there waiting for us. They were the sweetest people you could ever meet. I walked over and told them what the situation was, and they were very remorseful. I never spoke to Maurice after that day, but I still admire the Bee Gees for what they were able to do and the great music they created.

When Maurice passed away at the age of 53, I sent his wife and children a condolence letter. I never did get a reply. I live in hope that one day, in another place, I will get the chance to give that man a bear hug.

In our dining room today, there's the silver platter displayed that was a wedding gift to Mary and me from Richard and Karen Carpenter, who were also very good friends of the Osmonds. Our family were great fans of this talented brother and sister duo and their music. Karen had the sweetest singing voice, and her stage drumming inspired Jay to follow suit and become a drummer himself.

We would go to see them in their concerts, and they came to ours all the time. Their friendship was a blessing to us. Karen was a great friend to my brother Alan, and their relationship became quite serious, even to the point of almost getting married.

Despite this, we never really knew about her now well-documented problems with the eating disorder anorexia nervosa, which were attributed to the severe pressures of fame as well as her complicated family dynamics.

I do remember, though, having a very casual conversation about health issues generally and the pressures of performing and how exhausting it was to stick to schedules. Although anorexia was kept very quiet at the time, the disease plagued poor Karen for years until, tragically, she died in 1983 at the age of 32 from heart failure due to complications caused by it. So young, she was a huge loss to the music world. Even today, her work attracts great praise. Richard, apparently, had his own problems too.

Michael Jackson's own serious problems featured prominently in news outlets around the world. My own experience with him was much gentler, though still strange.

I was walking through the lobby of a Las Vegas hotel called The Excalibur on my way to see a show. Suddenly, I could hear a voice whispering: 'Merrill, Merrill…' I looked around but couldn't see anyone that the voice might belong to.

Then I spotted the door to what looked like a closet. Noticing that it was very slightly ajar, I walked over to it and peered inside. Through the crack, I could see Michael sitting there with another person I didn't recognize.

'Michael, what are you doing?' I asked.

'I'm hiding from security,' came the reply.

We both started to laugh, and I asked if I could do anything for him.

'No, I am just spending a little time here, getting away from everybody,' he added.

CHAPTER FOURTEEN

Clearly, he too knew how it felt to need to escape the pressures of fame now and then. Smiling, I shrugged my shoulders and continued on my way to see the show.

Other performers, like Elton John, who finally sought treatment for his own addiction in 1990 and beat it, have lived to tell their cautionary tales. Incidentally, there was a time years ago when the Osmonds were invited to socialize with the great star himself when we were in England. We agreed, but it never actually happened. As we were getting ready for the party he was hosting, he called back and said that he didn't recommend that we go along as we might feel uneasy!

After hearing the amusing story about the legendary late British chat show host Michael Parkinson's experience at a lavish party on Elton's yacht, maybe it's just as well.

The story goes that they arrived at the jetty minutes too late to board the yacht but were offered a ride out to it by a couple of water cops. But far from being welcomed aboard, guests were furious with them as, fearing an imminent police raid, they'd thrown their drug stashes overboard into the ocean! Needless to say, Parkinson, who has interviewed my brother Donny many times in the past, was not exactly popular at that party.

Someone I have a special relationship with is the West End theater actor Darren Day, whom I got to know through my charity work for the hearing impaired.

Despite his amazing talent and professional success—Darren (like Donny) starred in Andrew Lloyd Webber and Tim Rice's biblical musical Joseph and the Amazing Technicolor Dreamcoat—he has had his problems. In recent years, he has opened up about his struggles with addiction and admitted that he's 'lucky to be alive' after days of being hooked on cocaine and alcohol.

But once he got the right help and medication, he managed to turn his life around, and I just hope it's stayed that way. At the time, I wrote him a message saying: 'I just wanted to say how proud I am of you. You have been like a kindred brother to me. I will never forget you in this life or the life to come.'

It's true, I won't. And, like so many others who struggle as I have, he is in my prayers.

As you know, I take my faith very seriously and there have been many scary times when I have had to rely on it when performing with my brothers.

When we played for the first ever time at Madison Square Gardens, New York City, back in the 70s the atmosphere was absolutely unbelievable. The screams from fans were so loud that we couldn't hear ourselves sing and we couldn't even hear the band playing behind us.

We had to rely completely on the monitoring systems that sat on the floor in front of us. Even having those turned up as high as they would go, it was still tough to hear ourselves.

Our sound man who provided sound for many rock bands throughout his career said that our decibel or dB level, as it's called in the business, was the loudest he had ever heard. Louder even than rock bands like Led Zeppelin.

Because of occasional attempts by fans to attempt to reach us when up there performing, all of our own security as well as the police presence, were closely watching both sides of the stage.

Barriers were placed in front of the stage to keep the fans from being pushed or even crushed. Historically, pass out lines of fainting girls would occur if that happened.

The 20,000 people that filled the arena all seemed to have those little flash cubes on their cameras. These cubes were being pointed towards us, creating millions of little strobe lights. It was truly unbelievable.

CHAPTER FOURTEEN

As security staff were not watching the front of the stage, it obviously created an opportunity for someone determined enough to sneak past the barriers.

And as we started the song, 'One Bad Apple', I suddenly spotted a young man in a ripped T-shirt, holding a gun standing right in front of me while shaking almost uncontrollably. Being the lead singer, and standing right in front, I knew if anyone was going to get shot, it was probably going to be me.

Immediately, I went into one of those mental processes that I'd been taught by Chuck Norris to psych my opponent out. I stared right at this young man and never took my eyes off him.

Appropriately enough, the words of the song included: 'I can tell you've been hurt by that look on your face.'

It was a very choreographed number, but I didn't move a fraction. I just continued to stare at this young man. It seemed like forever, but I stayed completely still. Halfway through the song, security finally noticed what was going on and jumped on top of him. I don't know if my training from Chuck was what stopped the young man from shooting me, but it surely was a tense moment that I will never forget.

Doing our barbershop years, we would often travel around performing at county fairs and even rodeos. I'll never forget the day when our father had us all dressed up in white pants and red jackets. We were to perform during the half time segment of the rodeo.

I remember it was raining. Mud was everywhere and they had us arriving in a stagecoach. As soon as we were officially introduced, we came flying out into the arena. But we only got about 20 feet in and the wheels got stuck in the mud. We couldn't move. The applause obviously died down to nothing. We had no option but to get out of the stagecoach and make our way through the mud to the stage in the middle of the arena. I don't know how long it took us to get there, but it felt like forever. When we finally got there, our white pants were completely covered in mud.

Things went from bad to worse. It didn't help that there were only two microphones for the four of us and our three-piece band. Nevertheless, we started to sing a couple songs but as we were so far away from the crowd, we couldn't hear any applause. Then suddenly, the place started to roar with applause and loud yelling.

Relieved, I remember looking at the brothers and we all started smiling, thinking, 'Hey we're a big hit!' We then turned around to see a couple of big bulls that had gotten loose in the arena, and they were heading right towards us. Wearing the red jackets didn't help either. Suddenly we were a target and the crowd was roaring with excitement. But on we played...

Cowboys on horses, throwing their ropes everywhere, came charging in trying to catch these bulls before they got to us. We were right in the middle of a song and our drummer, who'd realized what was happening, started to speed up our song so fast we couldn't keep up with him!

They finally got the bulls just in time before they could hurt us. I remember writing in my journal that night, 'Why in the world didn't we take off our red jackets?' Good question but in the heat of the moment you don't always think straight. Talk about earning your dues! We more than earned our $60 that night.

In 1976, the brothers, Marie, and I performed at the Honolulu International Center in Hawaii. There were at least 18,000 people in the arena as I remember. The show began at 8:00pm. Fifteen minutes into it, the manager at the arena came running out on stage. He grabbed one of our microphones and yelled out to the audience that there was a bomb threat, and that everyone needed to evacuate the building immediately.

CHAPTER FOURTEEN

In that moment, our manager, Ed Leffler, came running on stage, grabbed the arena manager, and escorted him off quickly. I remember Ed yelling at that man saying, 'Are you crazy? Do you want a stampede in here?' The place went completely quiet. I don't remember seeing one person leave their seat. It was like they were waiting for us to make the decision.

Sitting in the first two rows of the arena were about thirty Mormon missionaries from our church, all dressed in their white shirts. We all looked at each other on stage, smiled, and said, 'We're staying.' It wasn't even a question. We had total peace of mind in that moment knowing that God would protect us. When we said that over the microphone, the place went crazy. The show went well. There were no issues at all.

However, when everyone had left the arena, the police came in and did a sweep of the building inside and out. They had police dogs sniffing out potential bombs that might have been placed. Well guess what? They did find an unexploded bomb, and it was right underneath our stage.

But the overriding peace of mind that we all felt on that stage, at that moment, overruled any feeling of anxiety we might have had. One thing that all my brothers and sister will say, is that when we all feel peace in a moment of decision, we know that we will be safe, and things will always turn out right. We've seen that happen over and over in our long career together.

Another fascinating experience happened in Malaysia when we were doing another concert there. The place was sold out and every seat was full except the front rows. Maybe 300 seats. One thing as an entertainer is that you really don't want to have empty seats up front. It's extremely noticeable and a bit awkward when you're trying to work an audience.

Around ten minutes before the show started, the security at the event came back into our dressing room and announced, 'We have a problem.' It was shocking to hear that a militant political movement had training camps throughout Malaysia, and they said that those empty seats were being filled right now by members of that organization. Honestly, we were shocked.

The question was immediately asked, 'Did we want to cancel the show?' I mean, seriously, were they there to take us out? That was the question seriously running through our minds. We all looked at each other and said, 'No, the show must go on.'

Now here's the real memory, throughout the show, they were the people that were dancing and singing the loudest. Seriously, they knew all the words to our hit records!

On a very different level of fear, I always felt nervous around Andy Williams, including on one occasion when we almost got fired. We were doing a concert with him at Indianapolis State Fair. Andy would bring us on and off throughout his show to be his background singers, but most of the time we would stay backstage hovering around a microphone to sing those backgrounds for him.

One day, the brothers and I thought it would be funny if during one of his songs we lowered from the lighting grid a plucked chicken that would hang about seven feet from the top of his head. We finally got the nerves to do it one day. As he was singing a beautiful ballad, down came the chicken.

What was supposed to be a very romantic love song turned into an hysterical crowd, laughing and crying out loud instead. Andy, being startled, began to look around to see why everyone was laughing. We saw him turn around and check his fly, thinking that it might be down.

CHAPTER FOURTEEN

And he had absolutely no idea what was hanging above his head. As a true professional, Andy kept singing his song, trying to regain his composure. Within time, we saw him look up and see the chicken. He slowly turned his head towards the side line of the stage and saw us laughing too.

All I can tell you is the glare that we got from him is still haunting us today. He never brought up that moment to us, but we had learned a most amazing and profound lesson. You don't do things like that to an extremely professional entertainer. Andy Williams was a serious and demanding entertainer. He was all about perfection. What we thought was funny, plain wasn't.

Another experience happened at the Ohio State Fair. We were standing behind Andy again singing background for him. During his final song, Moon River, something unique started to happen. When a nightly outdoor concert took place, it was hard to look into the audience because of the massive spotlights that would hit you in the eyes. One thing you could always see clearly was whatever was flying around inside those big white lights.

Well, the moment came for Andy's big final song to begin and we noticed something large flying around in this massive light. It finally became clear that it was a very large moth. And it seemed to be coming closer and closer to the stage every second. What was even a little scary was it seemed to have its target right towards Andy Williams.

Andy was singing the last two words 'and me' when that huge moth flew right into his mouth. He never sang those last two words as he was coughing up this big moth. Once again, the entire audience started laughing. We were a part of that laughter as well.

And once again, that piercing stare we got from him will never, ever be forgotten. You just do not do that to your boss, Andy Williams. He was extremely intimidating. And I understood very well how serious he was about his career, as a result of being a perfectionist myself. There's one thing to have a mistake made without anyone seeing it, but when it's seen by thousands and thousands of people while it's happening is another thing.

Chapter Fifteen

TROY DEAN, THE JELLY BEAN

Even before he was born on November 26, 1984, I knew that my beloved fourth son, Troy, would require my full support. I knew it for sure because he told me so.

Coming to me in a dream when Mary was pregnant, he said, 'Father, I'm going to need your help.'

In that same dream, I saw another child standing behind Troy. It was such a vivid dream that I never even thought to question it when I woke up. The first thing I did was turn to Mary and tell her that our son was going to need our help and that he would not be our last baby.

Things didn't work out exactly as I thought at that time because, with Troy's birth, Mary suffered from complications and needed to undergo surgery. There's always another way to do things, though. Our hearts and our family dining table had enough—more than enough—space for another child. So, happily, we adopted our wonderful second daughter, Sheila, making the prophecy come true. Troy was a toddler when She arrived to complete our family.

There was less than two years in age between them, and they enjoyed a close relationship. They did everything together and really shared a very special bond.

Troy was my best little buddy too, and I like to think that we shared a very special father-son bond. Our relationship was different from the one I had with my own father, but I took some lessons from my experience.

Mary and I believe that parenthood is part of our earthly test, and there's no doubt it is not easy. Our parenting styles were different, and it was never in doubt that Mary was the strict one and I was the soft one. I wanted to be the father that I had during my tenderest moments, like when my little canary, Melody, died, and he took me by the hand as we buried him together in the garden.

Of course, however hard I tried, I couldn't—just as my father couldn't—be like that all the time with any of my children because life and all its stresses get in the way. Deep down, I also realized that however much parents protect their children, there's simply no guarantee that bad things won't happen to them.

I knew that from my own experience of the abuse I had suffered at the hands of Ron Myers. How could that have ever happened when we were so guarded and protected? But it snuck in.

It was one of the worst experiences I could ever go through as a kid. People should not have to feel guilty because of someone else's actions. It took a lot of therapy to come to terms with it, even though it was always made very clear to me by my parents that I was in no way to blame. It's been a long, long journey that's been hard to understand.

While that abuse was not one of the problems Troy ever had to face, there were plenty of others, including many health problems. He struggled with debilitating headaches that could be so severe he needed to be hospitalized. Doctors prescribed heavy medication to

CHAPTER FIFTEEN

cope with the pain, and he relied on them so much that he became addicted to them.

Oh boy, was he right when he told me in that dream that he was going to need my help. It is too painful for me to go into any real detail about what happened because of his addiction problem, but it led to him serving a jail sentence. Visiting him in jail was the saddest experience I ever shared with him. That's all I can say on the issue.

Yet whenever he had any struggles as a child, adolescent, or adult, Troy nearly always managed to hide his pain behind such a beautiful smile. If I hadn't known what he was dealing with at any one time, I would never have guessed from his demeanor.

In our happy days, the two of us shared the same sense of humor, and we often laughed at things other people didn't find funny.

At other times, he could make anyone smile with his contagious laugh or one of his simple jokes. From the moment he was born, he was such a naturally bubbly, happy boy and a real joy to have around.

Always happy and always willing to help wherever he could, Troy got on with all five of his siblings, but he especially liked playing with his two sisters, Heather and Sheila, who were the closest in age to him. Within the family, he was known by his nickname, Troy Dean the Jellybean.

In his senior year, he received the honor of being made Student Body President. Everyone who met him loved him. He worked with the basketball team his junior and senior year, recording their numbers for the year. Academically, he maintained a 4.0 grade point average every year.

Being an Osmond, it probably won't surprise you to hear that he excelled at music, playing both the cello and the organ and he played these and the harpsichord for years every Christmas in the program called the Messiah. His goal was to become the Mormon

Tabernacle Choir organist. Hearing him play was like hearing angels sing—absolute heaven on earth.

His other interests included meteorology, and one of his other ambitions was to be a weather announcer on TV. But after school, he went to college with a view to becoming a Certified Nursing Assistant, which he achieved. That was always his main goal. He just loved helping others so much.

He also loved being around his family, especially at Christmas time. He was always known for keeping his Christmas lights up all year long!

He especially loved all 15 of his nieces and nephews, who were his pride and joy. He was a great uncle to them and loved being involved in their lives as much as he could be, always trying as hard as he could to share his own talents. He made each one of them feel special and made sure that they all knew how much he loved them.

In return, they all loved him and called him their 'favorite uncle.' Even on the days he was in pain, he wanted to be surrounded by his family.

Like his Uncle Wayne, he also had an interest in planes and aviation, but unlike Uncle Wayne, he never got to be a pilot.

Just days away from his 34th birthday, our Troy, suffered from dilated cardiomyopathy, despite not having a history of heart problems. He passed away in his sleep on November 9, 2018, in our family home in St. George, Utah. Sadly, I wasn't there, but Mary was.

I will never forget that last little embrace he and I had the night before I had to leave him to drive off to work the following day. I remember our final conversation. He was so tired, worn out, and was experiencing a tremendous amount of pain in his entire body.

In his weakened state, he still had a smile on his face and said goodnight to his old dad. That memory has been etched into my

CHAPTER FIFTEEN

brain for all these years since. Troy's funeral services were held on November 13th at noon in the Latter-day Saint Stake Center in St. George.

The day after his funeral, I had to be on the road in England for a whole tour, and people asked me, 'How are you able to do that?' I cried, obviously, and quite a bit, but I always knew he was standing next to me. He wanted me to keep going, to keep doing what I do.

As a faithful church member himself, Troy had served a full-time mission in London and in Louisville, Kentucky. He loved the gospel with all his heart, and it brought him peace and joy just as it has for me.

Oh boy, how I miss my son, though. I have wept buckets of tears as I remember all the good times, the laughs, and the deep conversations we had about this life and the life to come. We talked about why hard things happen to people who try to be good and help others. My son suffered with so many illnesses, and I don't know why. I've kept a record of our talks together. I've gone back and read many of them over the years.

The one journal entry I'll always cherish is the one where we both said if one of us were to die before the other, we'd promise to whisper to each other from the other side—to give special messages, impressions, or be allowed to come in a dream to continue our father-son relationship.

Even though the hole in my heart has not been healed, I can honestly say he has lived up to his promise. He's shown me in my dreams what he's doing, who he's working with, and how happy he is. He is not in pain anymore.

I guess this is why I'm writing this message. I know many of you will have lost a loved one and have suffered greatly. You might have lost faith and hope, even wanting to carry on; that the pain is too hard to handle. Maybe some of you even blame God for your loss.

The strength of my faith prevents me from doing that and believing that Troy will be with us for eternity keeps Mary and me going.

Tragically, Troy was not the first grandson of George and Olive to pass away young. In 2010, my sister, Marie, lost her 18-year-old son, Michael. As always, my beloved sister has been a great support in helping me deal with my loss. Having lived through similar pain herself, she has always understood exactly what I am going through.

Our shared belief in knowing where we are going to be when we pass away has helped immeasurably. I know that the days are getting closer and closer to when I will be able to hold Troy once again in my arms. I also know that he is happy and not struggling right now.

Before we are reunited, though, in the next life, our family has taken great comfort in learning from the examples that he set. On earth, like me, Troy was a great one for giving bear hugs. He welcomed everyone with one, along with a big warm smile. Everyone who knew him also knew that he loved them unconditionally; he was a friend to all.

Troy always used to ask me, 'Father, what is my mission? What am I here for?' I said, 'Son, you are going to change people's lives, and you don't realize it.'

Those words came true. Our family motto now is 'Troy harder.' Every day on his anniversary, we set aside time to 'Troy harder,' and it has changed our lives. His death changed the dynamics of our family. Whenever there's a little pride, wherever there's a little ego at stake, we remember that Troy had neither, and we say, 'Oh, Troy harder!' Now, to anyone struggling, I gently say the same: 'Troy harder,' and I know that if they do, they will be okay.

Chapter Sixteen

GLITTERING GALAS FOR GOOD CAUSES

On a summer evening in 2015, I found myself once again on stage singing 'Crazy Horses' to a wild crowd of fans. Nothing much new in that, you might think, except on this occasion, I was doing a duet with a very special guest, Susan Boyle.

It's well known that the Scottish singer who shot to fame on Britain's Got Talent has had health issues, but it was a magical moment for Susan and for me. Susan was thrilled; she's a lifelong Osmond fan and told us that in her teens, she slept with her head on a pillowcase imprinted with Donny's image. As a joke, I presented her with a pillowcase featuring my own image that Tracey had arranged earlier. Beyond excited, Susan announced to the audience, 'Out with Donny, in with Merrill,' and we all had a good laugh.

The occasion stands out in my memory because it embodies everything that The Annual Hearing Fund Gala, at which we were performing, is about. It's inclusive entertainment at its glittering best, but it's also a lot of fun, and most importantly, it's for a wonderful cause close to my own heart.

It was our mother's dream many years ago to raise awareness about deafness and help the hearing impaired throughout the world, following the arrival of my two older brothers, Tom and Virl, who were both born deaf.

Just before she passed away, appropriately enough on Mother's Day, May 9, 2004, our mother managed to whisper something important to me. She wanted me to continue the vital work that she had begun.

For 18 months previously, she had been living in a rehabilitation hospital following a severe stroke. Surgery was carried out at the Utah Valley Regional Medical Center in Provo, Utah, where, for two weeks afterward, she was left fighting for her life in the intensive care unit. Strangely, her younger brother, Tom, was fighting for his life in the next room following surgery for a perforated bowel.

While Tom never recovered, our mother did, though not fully. We all waited by her bedside and prayed for her to survive. Our prayers were answered, and it's with great pride that I look back and think that despite all her own physical health problems, she was still thinking of others in need. She truly died as she had lived her life.

Pride also comes from knowing that my second son, Justin, who was born 90 percent deaf, took over the reins from his grandmother, Olive, initially in the United States and later in the United Kingdom. It's fair to say that despite their hearing disabilities, Virl, Tom, and Justin could not have been luckier to have been born to the mothers that they were. Just as our own mother had worked tirelessly to ensure that her two eldest sons would lead full and normal lives, so too has Mary for Justin.

My brother Thomas Rulon Osmond arrived two years after Virl, on October 26, 1947. As toddlers, our mother used to let them play in the sandbox just outside their bedroom window. This left her free to go about her household chores, checking on them regularly.

CHAPTER SIXTEEN

One day, she knocked on the window to let them know she was watching them and became concerned when she noticed that Virl was the only one who would look up. He'd then touch Tom and point to our mother. They would both smile at her and then go back to their play.

It bothered our mother, so she did it several times more, and each time the same thing happened. Only Virl would respond to the knock. Piecing information together, she began to realize that Virl had been very slow in learning to speak, and his words were not very clear. He seemed to skip saying the 'r' and the 's' in his words. She also recalled times when she asked both boys to do something, and Virl would repeatedly stare at her the longest; she would often have to demonstrate to him what she meant. Tom always seemed distracted and uninterested in things that were said to him. It was always up to Virl to make eye contact with him and get the message across.

Talking it through with our father, they agreed to seek medical help. Mom called the school for the deaf in Ogden and arranged an appointment. Terribly anxious, they drove to the meeting with the audiologist at the school. Deep down, she knew that something was wrong. Waves of guilt swept over her as she recalled having German measles when pregnant with Tom and how Virl had been sick with them too. They'd also both undergone X-rays for another condition. Was this her fault in any way?

Tests were carried out, revealing that both boys suffered from severe hearing loss. Tom's was the worst, as he had an 87 percent decibel loss. Virl had a 75 percent decibel loss.

In total shock, our parents then had to listen to a doctor telling them, 'You might as well get used to the fact that your two boys will have to spend the rest of their lives in an institution.' In her journal, our mother wrote, 'What a cold, frightening feeling came over us. We were in a state of shock for days. Not our boys! The tests must be wrong. They were so healthy when they were born—it's a mistake!'

To make matters even worse for them, our mother was several months pregnant with their third child at that time. Concerned that her unborn baby would also be born deaf, she went to see her own doctor, who advised her not to have any more children, as they could all be born deaf. To her and our father's great relief (and later ours), our songwriting genius of a brother, Alan Ralph Osmond, was born free from any hearing defects on June 22, 1949.

Once our parents got over the initial shock and accustomed themselves to the idea that their two eldest boys were deaf, our mother added to her journal, 'We felt we just could not turn our sweet little boys over to an institution. We loved them too much.'

There and then, our mother's lifelong commitment to helping Virl and Tom, as well as learning as much as she possibly could about deafness, was formed. She also went on to support medical research into the condition.

When my mother first formed the Osmond Foundation, little did she know that her simple yet powerful concept would be taken by her daughter, Marie, and transformed into what is now known as the Children's Miracle Network. Through Marie's vision and dedication, that foundation has grown into a global force, raising billions of dollars and helping millions of children in need. What began as a mother's heartfelt desire to serve quietly became one of the greatest legacies our family has ever had the privilege of witnessing.

Despite being brought up with two deaf brothers in a loving environment where hearing problems were just a part of family life, I can't pretend that it wasn't a terrible shock when we discovered that our own little boy, born prematurely and weighing just five pounds, was also affected.

CHAPTER SIXTEEN

Unlike my own parents, I had known all along that the weakness was genetic, but I still never expected to see it surface in a child of my own. It was after noticing Justin's lack of response to certain sounds and loud noises that Mary and I took him to a doctor for tests. Upon learning of the diagnosis following the test results, we were devastated for days and left wondering how we would cope and provide him with the best life.

Memories of my own childhood proved a godsend after a time. I had always adored and admired my two older deaf brothers, who could skillfully do so many things that I couldn't in my early years, including milking Daisy the cow with perfect rhythm. They even taught the rest of us to tap dance.

Guided by our parents and coming from a home where the word 'disability' didn't exist, they had not been held back from achieving anything they set their minds to. Determined to mainstream them into a hearing world, our parents sent them for lessons at the local deaf school, but they were home to enjoy family life afterward, as opposed to spending their lives in an institution.

As I was away touring and recording, Mary was left with the task of attending to Justin's special needs, and she threw herself into it. Her educational background was a great advantage, and armed with the very latest research, she developed a preschool called 'A Child Shall Speak' for hearing-impaired and normally hearing pupils. Those with normal hearing acted as role models for those less fortunate, showing that children communicated through talking. The hearing-impaired children received speech therapy on a one-to-one basis.

We chose an auditory-verbal approach to communication rather than sign language, as my parents had chosen for my brothers. Slowly, over the years, he was patiently taught bit by bit how to use his voice, form words, and eventually speak. Justin responded well, going on to enjoy a successful mainstream education.

From 18 months old to age 22, he wore over-the-ear aids as well as a telecom box hung around his neck during elementary school. His teachers also wore a box around their necks, and their words went directly to his hearing aids. Once he'd stopped growing, he was fitted with hearing aids directly inside his ear canals.

As he grew, nothing stopped Justin, who also has the additional problem of having type 1 diabetes. He began learning to play the piano and viola and stuck with the viola, as it was easier for him to hear the lower tones. Also sporty, he played basketball and football, even competing on a national level. He won awards for math and completed his Eagle Scout award.

After graduating from Utah State University, he worked as a director of public relations for a company that makes and sells hearing aids. Part of his role has been to help organize humanitarian efforts for the hearing impaired in underdeveloped countries.

After meeting Tracey in Vegas and her agreeing to help him take his charity work to the UK, the first gala was launched in Leeds in September 2011, and the last in August 2022. It was produced every year by Justin and me, and took a huge amount of planning for months leading up to the event.

The family all supported this. Donny called in via Zoom at one event; Marie donated a doll from her vast collection for the auction and called in via Zoom; Jimmy, an incredibly talented artist, donated a wonderful painting he had done. Tom was a special guest, joining us for two galas and thrilling everyone with his spectacular dancing display. Alan, along with his sons David and Nathan, and brother Jay all joined us and performed over the years at the Gala weekend.

I have mentioned Susan Boyle, but there were many other celebrity guests eager to join us on those evenings. These included singing star Jane McDonald, whom I now consider a dear buddy, and comedians Cannon and Ball, who were hilarious, although I did struggle to understand their accents throughout the evening!

'Strictly Come Dancing' judge Craig Revel Horwood joined us, as did actors Shane Richie and William Roache, comedian Brian Conley, who was hilarious on stage, and the rock band 10cc, who were an amazing act. Jersey Nights, comedian Billy Pearce, singer Darren Day and many others. Shane donated a signed shirt that he'd worn on an episode of the BBC soap opera EastEnders. Afterwards, one fan offered Shane £50 for a kiss. Hesitating at first, he eventually agreed, as the money was for charity!

Darren Day became a good friend, and we spent many times talking about the Gospel. Many don't know but he is very spiritual, as I am, as this treasured message that he wrote referring to me reveals:

'Merrill is literally one of the best people I have met and become friends with. Not only is he an incredibly gifted performer, a true icon, he is also one of the most beautiful souls. Duetting 'Crazy Horses' on stage with him will forever remain as one of the highlights from my career. This may sound like a strange thing to say, but I feel closer to God when I'm in Merrill's presence.

Love you Merrill, Darren'

The event was originally hosted by broadcaster Fiona Phillips, a lovely lady and an original Osmonds fan, no less! I was devastated to learn years later that she has been diagnosed with Alzheimer's, like her own parents.

Former TV presenter Christine Talbot became our regular host, and she has become a dear friend of the family. Her true professionalism always shone through, and we felt so honored to have her support year after year. Christine also interviewed me in 2022 for 'My Life Story.'

Only once were we disappointed by a guest, and that was in 2013. I had personally invited Jermaine Jackson of The Jacksons fame to the Gala. He accepted, and we discussed the event at length.

We had all the programs printed, advertising his attendance at the gala, which was to be held at The Grand Theatre, Leeds. Tickets for it had sold out within days, and there was a lot of excitement surrounding the event. It was to be the first time an Osmond and a Jackson had performed together on British soil. It was advertised as 'the two lead singers together.'

It had been agreed, and everything was looking great, but there was a big hitch. Involved in a court case in the US, Jermaine apparently needed a judge's permission to leave the country. Suddenly, things went quiet, and on the morning of the gala, we discovered that he hadn't received the necessary legal clearance. In short, he wouldn't be attending but no one had called or let us know he hadn't boarded the plane.

We had to explain to the theater on the day of the show that Jermaine wasn't attending. They were legally responsible for putting a board outside the theater saying Jermaine wasn't attending 'due to unforeseen circumstances,' and offering a full refund to anyone who had bought a ticket. Luckily, not one person asked for a refund, even though we had complaints and a lot of disappointed people. I later emailed Jermaine and his manager asking for a donation to Justin's charity to try and cover the loss of flights, all the PR etc. but it never happened.

Another stressful time was when 20 Virgin Atlantic pilots turned up in full uniform to attend as my special guests! I had invited them on the spur of the moment, as I was always treated like royalty by the crew and invited into the cockpit after each flight whenever I flew over to England.

I guess I hadn't thought it through, and I hadn't really expected them to take up my offer. But 20 minutes before the curtain went up, the theater manager frantically called to inform us of their arrival,

CHAPTER SIXTEEN

and we were already sold out! Somehow, seats were found for them upstairs, and the show started on time. Panic over!

Generally, though, most events ran smoothly. After each one, we would all breathe a sigh of relief, totally exhausted but incredibly proud of what we had all achieved. To see the children benefit made all the hard work more than worthwhile.

We sponsored many children over the years, providing music lessons, musical instruments, swimming lessons, dancing lessons, or whatever that child dreamed of but couldn't otherwise do due to their hearing problems and lack of funding. Some of the children would then return and perform at the gala with Justin, which for me was a true highlight. To see the improvement and growth in these children each year was just wonderful. They and their families became family to us over the years.

In the USA, we provided free hearing aids for children, but in the UK, these are available on the National Health Service, so we helped them in other practical ways.

In 2013, we were approached by a newspaper to conduct an interview with a deaf British lady named Joanne Milne. Brave Joanne went on to become a dear friend of the family and worked closely with us at each Gala.

A YouTube video clip captured a sobbing Joanne as her cochlear implants were switched on. That short emotional video became one of the world's most-watched videos of 2014. This catapulted Joanne into the public eye, and she has since been on an incredible journey of sound. All that time, her world was getting darker by the day due to her having Usher Syndrome.

Joanne now has 95% sight loss, yet is married and the proud mother of two beautiful children. Despite her disabilities, she continues to work tirelessly with her own charity. She became a valued part of our operations team and featured in many award-winning documentaries, using her high-profile status to raise awareness and carry out humanitarian work to improve the lives of many deaf and deaf-blind children all over the world.

Joanne became an amazing ambassador for The Hearing Fund and promoted the charity in all her work as she became more well-known throughout the world. We were proud to partner with her on a trip to Bangladesh, which was televised by the BBC. Joanne flew out and helped by donating and fitting 508 children with hearing aids. Many of these families had walked for days to see Joanne.

The BBC premiere was attended by many keen to hear the uplifting story of how hundreds of young lives have been changed. It was very emotional to watch these young children hear their mothers' voices for the very first time.

This was a heartwarming trip, because we also gave the 500+ children and teens a three-year supply of batteries for their hearing aids. So, we were very disheartened to hear later that the parents had sold the batteries for food. What a sad situation…

We were in awe of all that she has achieved and the way that she has never let her deafness and blindness stop her from achieving her goals.

Personally, I am grateful to everyone who has helped make each of the Galas the success they were. Especially, all the volunteers who worked tirelessly on the team to ensure the event ran smoothly. In 2022, though, we felt that it had run its course and it was time to hold the final one.

Of course, none of these 11 star-studded Galas would have ever happened in the first place had it not been for Justin. I am so proud of him and what he has achieved. Had he not been born deaf, he would not have been able to help thousands around the world by providing hearing aids they would never have had otherwise. He truly is my miracle boy.

Chapter Seventeen

SERENITY

When Elvis told me all those years ago in Vegas that if he had to do it all over again, he would go out into the audience and shake hands with everyone, it really affected me. I took his words on board and since then it's what I have always tried to do.

It's not always possible but anyone who knows me, will understand where I am coming from. I love nothing more than being among people—family, friends, fans, even total strangers—and to be able to wrap my arms around them. That's me. As scientists are proving more and more, we all need human touch.

It's the most basic of our needs. As well as reducing stress and anxiety, it improves our mood and enhances our feeling of belonging. Physically, it's believed that it can also help reduce blood pressure and strengthen our immune systems.

New research by public health researchers at Harvard University has even shown that chronic loneliness in adults aged over 55 might increase the risk of stroke by as much as 56 per cent.

And that's on top of previous studies that have linked loneliness to a higher risk of developing cardiovascular diseases. It's magic!

My Serenity program has been my way of combining my lifelong desire to heal people and music.

Tracey and I initially discussed the concept of Serenity in 2012 and we later launched the first one in a spa hotel in Grantham, England, in the Spring. It was such a wonderful success that it became an event that we held every year—both in the UK and the US.

At these weekend-long events, I have had the chance to talk to people on a very personal level; something that was impossible to do in the bubble that I lived in during the seventies.

Many of the people that I have been able to connect with at Serenity events were actually fans in the seventies who didn't have a hope of getting to know the real me back then. Nor me them.

Over the years, we have had some amazing motivational speakers who would talk about anything ranging from physical health and wellbeing to dealing with personal traumatic life experiences. My own beloved son, Troy, was one of the speakers who opened his own beautiful heart so movingly, bringing tears to many eyes, including mine.

Donny and other members of my family called in to talk with our guests via a Zoom link. So did Michael Jackson's older brother, Tito, who was an original member of the Jackson 5 and went on to achieve great success as a singer, songwriter and musician.

Interestingly, like our own mother, Tito's mother was a religious woman though she did not follow our faith. She was also musical and played the piano and clarinet.

As much as it had quite a serious side, we also managed to keep it fun. All the weekends were held in spa hotels so that guests could relax and have spa treatments too.

We staged armchair yoga, duck herding and dance sessions as well as nature walks over the years. On the Saturday night, I would

CHAPTER SEVENTEEN

always perform a private Serenity concert. If it was taking place in the UK we would have special dinners, and in Florida, where the weather could usually be guaranteed, we organized a barbecue concert.

One year we had the celebrity TV chef and author Kwoklyn Wan join us. We'd met at the BBC studios previously and got on really well.

In case you didn't know, he's the brother of the style guru Gok Wan, but is also very successful in his own right.

I even put an apron on myself, grabbed a wok and attempted to cook a stir fry. It was great fun but, needless to say, I doubt I'd ever have been asked to give up my day job and become a chef!

When we staged a Serenity in Nevada in 2017 we even had a wedding! It was an outdoor event in a beautiful poolside location and I was honored to be asked by the bride to walk her down the specially created aisle. I think we all enjoyed that event.

These events were hugely popular, and tickets always sold out within days of going on sale. I always wanted to limit them to 100 guests to maintain the concept and vision that I'd had in the first place. I'm not sure everyone understood why we limited the numbers, especially as there was always a waiting list, but I really didn't want to lose that personal touch. That was the whole point of Serenity.

One, now funny, event was in Mesquite, Nevada in September 2017. This was a great venue with the huge backdrop of mountains 80 miles north of Las Vegas. We had planned a day trip to see Zion Park for the day, but the coach company unexpectedly went into liquidation just two days beforehand. They informed us just the day before the trip and we desperately tried to hire another coach.

It wasn't looking promising at this late stage as there was a big boxing match taking place in Vegas, so all transport companies were already fully booked. Eventually, though, we found a company who could assist us but on the way to Zion the bus overheated and broke down on the busy freeway.

It was very hot, and the bus didn't have any bottled water on board.

The poor driver was a young girl who didn't know how to help 60 middle aged ladies, some of whom had mobility issues, that were stranded on the side of the freeway in the baking heat.

Troy, Tracey and I were following on in a car, so we stopped and made several calls but the only thing we could really do was offer reassurance that a replacement bus was on its way, but we were told that wouldn't be for at least two hours.

Our trip to Zion was looking less and less likely now. The guests that had already gone ahead by car had arrived there and would be waiting for us.

Taking Tracey and Troy to a local Walmart store, we bought lots of supplies of bottled water, candy, fruit—and a frisbee!

I don't know what I was thinking but at the time it seemed a good idea to lighten the mood. Needless to say, no one played frisbee by the side of a very busy road.

As it began to look less and less likely that the replacement bus would be there any time soon, I made an urgent call to my church and asked if anyone could help. I was getting concerned not only about the safety but whether the replacement was even going to arrive at all.

I am so grateful to them for saving the day. They arranged for several minibuses and vans to collect guests and take them back to the hotel. Members of the church were amazing and we were so grateful for their help as they all arrived one by one to our aid. Our wonderful day trip planned to Zion never happened though.

I have to admit that I was expecting to hear many complaints from the guests, but it turned out to be quite the opposite. Back at the hotel that night, they told me what a wonderful experience it

CHAPTER SEVENTEEN

actually had been as they had all bonded just sitting there by the side of the busy road doing nothing except share stories. Some had used white stones to write Osmond names on the grass banking at the roadside.

In the end it felt as if it had happened for a reason. It is a strong belief of mine that things always do and my 'no accident theory' had been proved right again on that roadside where lots of bonding and breakthroughs had happened that day.

If my wish, like Elvis's, was to engage more with people, it was certainly granted with Serenity.

Chapter Eighteen

WHEN THE SHOW COULDN'T GO ON

Like everyone else, when the world started to talk about a virus spreading rapidly around the world in 2020, we thought it would probably last no longer than three weeks and wouldn't be any more serious than flu.

That year was planned to be a particularly busy one for me. My schedule was full of over 40 dates scheduled in England plus US dates and of course the all-important annual gala weekend. I felt a blessed man to still be this busy at 66 years of age and I was a happy man.

When I left Las Vegas for Heathrow on March 11, I was feeling totally relaxed about Covid-19 as everyone was at that time. In fact, most people thought it would be a disruption mostly affecting China. If only we'd known…

As time went by, concern around the world escalated as people began dying from this unknown virus for which there was no vaccine at this stage.

I was excited to have a sold-out tour ahead of me in England beginning on March 13 at Hunstanton, Norfolk. This was always a popular venue and one where I had performed many times. More dates followed in quick succession at Butlins, Skegness, Billingham, Milton Keynes, Birmingham, London, Eastbourne, Yeovil and Torquay. Between May and October another 21 concerts were scheduled.

I opened the tour at Hunstanton and, as a precaution, I wore gloves on stage which I changed after each show.

I canceled all the Meet and Greet events and there was no more hugging the fans at stage doors. This wasn't a legal requirement; in fact, the theaters were all still fully open and it was business as usual, but I decided we would take these measures to act responsibly and protect the team around me for the long tour we had ahead of us.

This time it felt very strange. While fans were still up close to the stage, singing and dancing close to each other as they always did, I didn't reach out into the audience as I usually love to do.

We were watching the news daily, in fact there were updates hourly at that time. Our promoter, Tony Denton, was keeping a close eye on the situation concerning the theaters.

Suddenly, we had a handful of people posting on our social media saying we were being irresponsible and asking why I wasn't canceling the tour and accusing me of not taking it seriously.

One person posting quite accusingly was actually present at all the shows! Tracey was receiving lots of messages accusing her of putting lives at risk even though it was out of her hands. And mine for that matter. The problem we had was that it wasn't our decision. We couldn't cancel the shows as we were contracted for them and if I pulled out, we would be in breach of contract. It was as simple as that. Until British Prime Minister Boris Johnson closed the theaters, we had to continue.

CHAPTER EIGHTEEN

Our promoters and agents were indeed encouraging all their acts to follow the guidelines and that meant 'the show must go on' until the Government stepped in and declared otherwise.

We had lots of people depending on income from this tour and everyone wanted to follow Government rules so that any insurance wouldn't be void for the band, crew, theater staff etc; it became a serious responsibility for everyone.

The UK Government was still saying it was perfectly safe for theaters to remain open and indeed were encouraging people to support their local theaters. So, we continued but taking extreme caution and staying as safe as we could with the gloves, no Meet and Greets, lots of hand sanitizer and of course boxes of masks. I didn't mind wearing the masks, when not performing, and began calling myself Zorro as at that time, I felt safe and not overly concerned. Hundreds of other performers, like me, were still continuing their shows throughout the country and playing to huge audiences, some in arenas.

The second show at Butlins, on March 14, was always sold out to an audience of over 3,000, usually fans of the 70s music. We performed there to an audience, who absolutely was on fire! The electric atmosphere in the holiday camp always creates a fun venue to perform but this show seemed even more so.

The following day was a travel day then the next show was in Billingham on March 16. Again, it was a venue I have performed at many times, both solo and with my brothers. The manager told us she was starting to get concerned as people were suddenly getting nervous about attending crowds and were either asking for refunds or just not turning up for shows they had booked. But despite her concern, we were nearly sold out again to a very enthusiastic crowd and it was another great show.

The venue assured us they were remaining open until the UK Government said otherwise. In fact, while I was performing on stage that night, it was suddenly announced by the BBC that all theaters had to close that night at midnight for at least three weeks. So that was the end of the tour.

President Trump had announced on March 14 that the UK would be added to America's travel ban and it would take effect from March 16 but American citizens would still be allowed to travel home to the US so I wasn't overly concerned at that stage.

Tracey was talking to the airlines hourly, trying to get me home as they were suggesting stopping all flights if the numbers of Covid-19 cases kept increasing at the rate they were. Tracey booked me on a flight but then we would get a notification an hour later saying it had been canceled! This happened on four separate occasions and my family were getting concerned too as they had heard the UK would be going into lockdown soon and I wouldn't be able to get home in time. In the end we made the decision to just drive to Heathrow and stay there until I could get on a flight home.

On one of the last flights to leave Heathrow on the evening of 18th March, I headed home. It was a surreal time in the airport as everyone was trying to get home. I was flying direct to Las Vegas, but we had to divert and land in Los Angeles as the air traffic control tower in Las Vegas had several people with Covid-19 and they were re-directing any planes due to land there. This was now getting serious. After all the extreme caution I had taken on the tour in England and here I was now sitting on a shuttle bus taking everyone to Las Vegas from Los Angeles airport. Fortunately, I didn't catch Covid-19.

The world was now thinking it would be a three-month problem so Tracey and Tony Denton, my promoter, started to reschedule all the tour dates we had had to cancel. This proved a logistical nightmare as every performer was doing the same thing and the theaters were

CHAPTER EIGHTEEN

always booked up in advance. The theater admin staff were all working from home but tried to reschedule the dates we requested. They were, in fact, moved at least three more times after this as the virus peaked in various countries and all flights were grounded.

Lockdown was a time for me to return to my writing and I also started painting again, two of my lifelong passions.

In November I was offered the chance to do a live stream in London that would be filmed and streamed around the world. There was so much excitement for this from fans who had missed seeing live performances and this was one way that we could do that.

The first time I returned to England after Covid-19 was on November 19 that year to do the live streaming in Islington, London. This was a very tight and strict proviso that there were no audience or visitors from outside the film crew and our team. It was classed as a filming as we had a production company to stream it worldwide and later put it on a DVD.

We had to have a special filming permit as live concerts still weren't allowed and we all had to always stand three feet apart on marked places on the stage and wearing masks apart from when performing. I also had to have several Covid PCR tests before I could fly, when I landed, and again before I left for home. This was the start of many precautions I would have to have to return to performing. Everyone then had to isolate for five days after the filming.

I believe I was the first US performer to return to England after Covid-19. You had to have a special work permit to travel and the airport was eerily quiet. On arrival, I had to quarantine for five days and take another PCR test before I could join the team for the filming.

Masks had to be worn everywhere, and we had to create a team bubble, being careful not to mix with others. Only certain hotels were allowed to open, and restaurants were still closed. It was a strange feeling in London to see it so quiet as we all traveled to and from the venue. We weren't allowed to travel anywhere else due to the filming permit restrictions. It was strictly to the hotel and venue only.

The streaming was held in Bush Hall, a beautiful theater in vibrant West London. Security was obviously tight as we had to ensure no one entered the building who wasn't on our permit. Covid-19 testing had to be carried out daily on everyone as per the permit. No one was allowed in the building who weren't on our permit list.

It sure felt unreal to sing to cameras with no live audience to interact with, but it was a great opportunity to sing with my band again and it felt like a step back to normality. Thousands of fans watched the streaming worldwide and it was a huge success, allowing everyone to watch a 'concert' from the comfort of their own home.

I was literally overwhelmed by the response after the streaming on my social media. I knew then it was the right decision, and all the planning and strict rules were worth it for fans to see a live concert again after the lockdown.

Brother Donny posted on social media on November 12th. 'Glad to see my brother, Merrill, finding a way to share his music and bring people together through a live streamed concert.'

I was glad too during what was such a testing time for everyone round the world.

Chapter Nineteen

A LIFE'S MISSION

We were always told that the Osmond brothers were serving a lifelong mission for our church through our music and performances. I believe this to be true as I still meet so many people who joined the church through our testimonies.

Mary and I had always hoped to serve a senior mission for our church, The Church of Jesus Christ of Latter Day Saints, and from April 2023 – April 2024 we were working together on a 12 month mission at The Washington DC Temple Visitors' Center, greeting thousands of people six days a week, 365 days a year.

We were living in a little apartment about 15 minutes from the visitors' center. We usually worked five hours a day, although during December it was ten hours a day. We served with some wonderful people there who will always remain close friends to us. Mary kept count of all the countries that she personally met visitors from, and it numbered 85 different countries by the end of the mission.

Mary says, 'Every day I woke with a purpose to spread the gospel. We met people that were so amazing and that we have become good friends with. It was hard but so, so rewarding.'

There were those that were just curious to see what the temple was and what we believed. Others would come in and want to just argue and try to create a lot of drama about various beliefs.

Mary and I were walking on sacred ground every day for an entire year. On a personal level, I found it humbling that so many people from all around the world would walk into the visitors' center and immediately recognize me. They didn't always know which Osmond I was, but they knew I was one of the brothers. Ambassadors and delegates would visit from many countries around the world.

A memorable incident occurred when a gentleman walked in, visibly upset, and holding the Koran. He was from Iraq and began telling everyone how deceived we were. Our job as senior missionaries was to engage with him. When I approached him, he looked at my name badge and was stunned. 'Are you an Osmond?' he asked. I replied, 'Yes, I am. I've been the lead singer of The Osmonds for many years.' His demeanor changed instantly. He told me he was one of my biggest fans and that during the 70s, every one of our records reached number one on their radio stations.

What could have been a tense moment turned into a two-hour conversation about why the Osmonds have lasted for so many years. I had the opportunity to show him around the center and discuss the life of Jesus Christ. When he left, we shared a hug, and I saw a tear in his eye. 'I'm coming back,' he said. 'I want to know more. I want to understand this feeling. I haven't felt anything like this since I was a child.' A truly cool story, indeed.

This reminds me of a strange story that we heard from the CIA after they had carried out Operation Red Dawn to capture Saddam Hussein in Iraq in 2003. The military found a series of Osmond albums from the 70s amongst his belongings. I don't know if that's a good story or a bad one!

CHAPTER NINETEEN

Life was so hectic back in the 70s that we never really knew where our music was being played so it's interesting to find out now. Countless visitors at the center told me that they had listened to us from their homes in Syria, Pakistan, Jerusalem, and China to name just a few.

For both Mary and me, our mission was truly a life-changing experience. Quite apart from its religious significance, if I ever needed any proof that Elvis had had the right idea when he mentioned the importance of meeting and embracing people, this was surely it.

Chapter Twenty

IT'S HARD TO SAY GOODBYE

During my goodbye US concert in April 2022, I found myself in the dressing room of the old Las Vegas Hilton Hotel and what a truly humbling moment it was.

This was where we'd first met Elvis back in the early seventies when the Osmonds were about to hit the big time.

Since those early days, there's been a name change, and it's now called The Westgate Resort where Barry Manilow has a residence.

It's still got the largest stage in town and it's where I was performing two special concerts to officially end my long showbusiness career in the United States.

Appropriately located near Elvis Presley Boulevard, this was Elvis' home away from home during his long residency. The King of Rock 'n' Roll captivated audiences in the hotel's legendary showroom from 1969 to 1976.

In the hotel lobby there's a statue of Elvis, capturing his charismatic stage presence. It's a tribute to his extraordinary talent and influence on the Vegas entertainment scene.

As I walked humbly around The King's dressing room, backstage and private rooms where we met so many stars, it brought back a million memories for me and stirred so many emotions.

We didn't only meet Elvis in these rooms. There were lots of other big names that we were introduced to here too: Dean Martin and Frank Sinatra, for example.

It was also here, at the Lake Tahoe casino, where the Swedish American actress Ann-Margret experienced a major fall in September 1972, when she fell from an elevated platform to the stage and suffered serious injuries including a broken left arm, cheekbone and jawbone.

Ann-Margret was Elvis's co-star in 1964's Viva Las Vegas playing the part of Rusty Martin who wowed audiences with her performance. She and Elvis were apparently dating for a time.

Coming full circle, I started out there with my brothers in the seventies and I was ending it there in 2022. It felt like such an honor and so fitting to be performing there on this special occasion.

This place is where it all happened. It felt like yesterday.

I held a fan gathering in the afternoon, attended by hundreds of loyal fans.

These are always special events but this one was particularly special for me and I hope for the fans too who had traveled to share the moment with me. Over the years, we have grown up together and now it was ending and we were saying goodbye.

After the buffet, my son Shane had arranged for more than 300 delicious candy caramel apples to be delivered at the get-together and my grandchildren were wandering round the room handing them out. It made it a real emotional family affair from the start.

As Mary and I sat on 'thrones' on stage, we took part in a fun Question and Answer session with the fans. Then it was my grandchildren's turn to join me on stage. What an incredibly moving

CHAPTER TWENTY

moment it was when they sang 'God Be with You Until We Meet Again.' What a highlight and one that has run through my mind so many times since. When I went to bed later that night, I just stared at the ceiling for hours, reliving every moment like this one as Mary slept peacefully beside me.

For the evening performance itself, I had also invited around 200 family members and friends to join me in leaving the US world of showbusiness behind. It was never going to be easy...

Donny and his wife, Debbie, and family were among them and I learned afterwards that Donny's intention was to 'just be a fan' that night. It made me laugh because at the very height of Osmondmania, he was the one who heavily disguised himself as an old man and before The Osmonds were due to go on stage, he sat in the show's audience with all the fans! Just imagine what their reaction would have been had they only realized! As it was, he was up on his feet singing, dancing and taking pictures on his phone on my big night.

At the end of my set, I was finishing the show with the song 'It's Hard to say Goodbye'—an emotional song that captured the evening perfectly.

It truly was the end of an era and the moment when Donny came up behind me and gave me the biggest brotherly hug, gave me the strength to continue. He truly understood how I was feeling at that time as only Donny could.

Suddenly, everybody was capturing that moment on their camera phones and that photograph of the two of us went viral on social media.

The following day, Donny posted it on social media with a message saying: 'It was a night that I will never forget.'

Me too, brother!

I was touched by the kind words that he spoke about me. It truly was the end of an era.

Earlier I had also invited my son Travis to join me up on stage to play 'Hold Her Tight' with me. Travis is a great bass player, and it was such a special moment we shared on stage.

Throughout the show, tribute videos from many stars were playing behind me which really touched my heart.

The Queen of Country herself, Dolly Parton, who I have huge respect for as a performer and a person, was one of them. Although we've never performed together, our paths have crossed many times over the years.

In her inimitable style, her voice boomed out saying:

'Well hi, Merrill, are you finally going to retire after sixty years? What's up with you?

I'm still at it! I'm as old as you are, probably older.

I just wanted to say congratulations on your retirement. We all love you. You have added so much to the Osmond family but to the whole world in general. You have written so many wonderful songs.

You play so great; you're a great producer. You've done so much that a lot of people don't even know about.

Hey Merrill, guess what? I will always love you. Dolly'

An emotional Marie, fondly known as my 'favorite' sister, couldn't be there because it coincided with a holiday cruise that her son and his wife had bought her and husband Steve for Christmas.

'Hi my cute brother! Well, I am not there as you can see and I have to tell you I am so sad to be missing this special occasion. I would so be there, Merrill, if I could.

I send you my deepest love and huge congratulations on a tremendous, remarkable six-decade career. If anybody deserves a moment like this, you do, my big brother. I love

CHAPTER TWENTY

you eternally but you already know that. You have brought so much joy and happiness to countless people throughout the world over the years and I just want you to have an amazing time and I will see you soon. I love you, Bear.'

As well as being in the audience, our little brother Donny also had his turn saying:

'This is crazy. I can't believe these are your last shows. Absolutely crazy. You know, it's been an honor to work with you over the years and to sing with you and to dance with you and to perform with you, work with you. Just to be called your brother is an honor. And you've been my mentor. Yes, it took every single one of us to create The Osmonds but it was you as the lead singer that created the sound of The Osmonds and we will never forget that.

I love you.'

Watching all the tribute videos from friends such as Chuck Norris brought tears to my eyes.

Chapter Twenty One

A MAN LIKE ME

So, who is the real Merrill Davis Osmond? I suppose I could say that I am officially Dr. Merrill Davis Osmond or Sir Dr. Merrill Davis Osmond!

I've already told you about my honorary doctorate, which gave me the title that brought tears to my eyes because I've dreamed of having it since I was a little boy. Unfortunately, the medical career that I wanted along with it wasn't part of the package, but through my Serenity work, I hope I've promoted some healing of a different sort. It gave me the opportunity to share my personal stories about the struggles I've gone through and, hopefully, bond with those who might be struggling themselves with those same issues.

Among those who attended, I experienced many breakthroughs that had been kept inside for years, causing them tremendous health issues, anger issues, and mental conditions that prevented them from having peace of mind.

That's why I loved Serenity. It was all about the one-on-one opportunity to bare my soul and, in my own way, be a healer of hearts. When we all became one at the end of Serenity, the spirit of goodness was felt throughout the room.

I would often sing a few songs and create what I felt was a healing mechanism through music. Through music, intertwined with uplifting lyrics, the heart can be opened, and good things can come from that.

I hope that the thousands of people who attended Serenity will remember what they felt and what they learned. The feedback I have received over the years has been overwhelming. Those who attended were literally able to change directions and bring more happiness and joy into their lives.

If Serenity only helped one person throughout the years, then I know that the vision I saw years ago was all worth it.

I held my last Serenity in England in September 2024. This was an emotional event but I truly think it was one of the best we have done. My son Travis joined me.

I posted this message to the guests attending that weekend.

My dear Serenity friends,
Thank you all for allowing me to be a part of your journey for all of these years. I hope that our time together has inspired you to take charge of your life and embrace change. Remember, every day is a new opportunity to grow and evolve. I have faith that you will overcome any challenges that come your way and continue to spread love and positivity.

Stay true to yourself and never forget that you are capable of achieving greatness.

But remember, it is important to also take care of yourself and prioritize your mental and emotional well-being. Don't be afraid to reach out for support and take breaks when needed. You can overcome any challenge and create a brighter future. Keep believing in yourself and never forget that you are capable and worthy of all the love and happiness in the

CHAPTER TWENTY ONE

world. Let love guide you and embrace the serenity that comes with inner peace.

You're truly loved, Merrill

I have also been knighted twice. Once was by the Order of Saint Michael of the Wing and received Vatican approval from the Pope. The other knighting was The Knights Templars.

Despite Donny, who attended my graduation with me, jokingly asking on social media, 'Does this mean I'm required to bow each time I see him?', I'm still just plain old me. No bowing required unless I'm doing it myself at the end of a concert.

It's never been hard for me to stay grounded about success. If it were, I'd only have to remind myself that my lack of formal education and qualifications means that if I had to go out today and get a real job, I'd probably end up digging holes in the ground for caskets.

I'm not saying there's anything wrong with doing that; we need people to do that job. It just wasn't an ambition I ever had. To be brutally honest, digging those holes for caskets would require a lot of strength that I probably no longer have at my age anyway.

I don't want to point the finger of blame at anyone for my basic education. Some of my brothers did go on to gain academic qualifications. Nobody became a medical doctor, but Wayne achieved the other ambition I had and became an accomplished pilot. I've always been so proud of him for that. I can't tell you how much I loved sitting in a Learjet flying at 40,000 feet in the air with him as the pilot. It was a highlight of my life that I will never forget. Especially now that it cannot be repeated.

Maybe the extreme anxiety that I have suffered made me too fearful and exhausted to train and chase those goals. One important lesson that I have learned, though, is that maybe I tried too hard… Sometimes I wouldn't—or often couldn't—be honest with people. I wouldn't say what I was really thinking about things. A lot of the time, when I'd find myself in a tricky situation, I'd calmly say, 'You know what, you are right,' when all the time I knew that they were not right. I just wanted to avoid any sort of confrontation.

I know now that trying to keep the peace and please everyone put a lot of pressure on me. Heck, I sure tried hard to keep everybody happy and that's taken its toll on my mental health.

Even in the seventies, I was always thought of by anyone who came close to the Osmonds—staff, colleagues, journalists—as 'the laid-back one.' Really, though, without even being aware of it myself, I was internalizing my anger, and that's not good for anyone's mental well-being.

At seventy-one, it's finally dawned on me that it's impossible to please everyone all the time. I know that now. If there's a disagreement, you do not just roll over and take whatever mud is thrown at you. You can still be calm and nice while being firm as well. I can look back and see that a lot of that people-pleasing has been responsible for my stress, anxiety, and manic episodes.

These days, I can process and voice my negative thoughts much better than I ever could, and I've come around to believing that the career path I have trodden was meant to be. It has shaped me into the man I am today. And I hope that by reading this book, you have a good idea of who that man really is.

Yes, I am the shy, anxious lead singer of the Osmonds who never wanted to be in that position because of all the attention that it drew to me. It was a unique and often quite a lonely position to be in, but despite all the problems it caused me, I have experienced such great joy from it, working with such an amazing group of brothers. I couldn't have asked for a better career.

It wasn't just the big awards and gold records that made me proud either. There were simpler moments too when we excelled

CHAPTER TWENTY ONE

at what we did that made us proud. Like the time I was performing with my brothers in Mexico City in a big coliseum with a sold-out audience. The power suddenly went out and never came back on. We had a choice: to cancel or to do what we have always done—keep the show going on. So, we sang barbershop harmony for a whole hour. To be able to switch from a full show that was prepared to do an a cappella show took all the brainpower the four of us had. The standing ovation we received at the end of it went on for more than ten minutes. What a moment that was.

Other stage disasters could not be saved quite so smoothly and successfully. I'll never forget the moment when we were performing with Bertha and Tina, an elephant act in Reno, Nevada. It was quite a day!

They opened the show for us, and at the end of their act, they would leave the stage, and we were to run on singing our opening number. What we didn't realize was that the elephants had left us a present on stage—a huge pile of dung right in front of our microphones!

The audience was dining on lobster and steak right in front of the stage, and because of the smell, they started walking out. Our intro was playing for a good five minutes until two guys came out on stage and carried out a 'whistle while you work' routine, scooping up all that stuff and calmly putting it into a wheelbarrow. We did finish the show. If there's one thing you can count on, it's that the Osmonds will always work out a problem when performing on stage. But it was terrible—just terrible!

At times, there were other members of the family who wanted to be me. I was put down by them despite being the creator of it all in many ways. It really hurts my heart, and it has created a lifetime of dilemmas for me.

While I get a definite spark from being out there performing, I truly still don't relish the fame that goes with the job. It detests me when I see someone in the pursuit of fame and fortune pushing everyone out of their way to do it. I am just not that kind of person.

Believe it or not, for somebody who loves music as much as I do, I don't sing in the shower at home, and I don't even like singing in church! To me, it is very much a job. One that I've loved and hated, but hey, I've survived! Now, when I am on stage with the band creating the sound I now have with my Dream Team, it's a different story. I wish I had found these guys years ago and I tell them that often!

They truly have shown me professionalism, loyalty, and a dedication that I have never known before. With them everything is in place when I arrive. They know me so well, and this gives me so much reassurance. I am at peace instead of being stricken with the anxiety I always used to get before a show years ago.

That's not to say that I don't struggle when I come off stage and receive accolades afterwards. Old habits really do die hard, and even when I get a five-star review for a show, I struggle to accept that they are meaning me. How can I receive that accolade when I was told that I would never succeed without my brothers behind me?

I was always discouraged from going solo as I thought I would fail, but in recent years, my solo career has been amazing. I have enjoyed it immensely, and I am more relaxed going on stage and being on stage than I ever have been before.

If there's one thing I've learned, it's that you can never build your happiness on someone else's unhappiness. If you think you can tear someone down a little and it will somehow miraculously lift you up, you're being blinded by jealousy. If you think that if you're negative enough, you can keep everyone else down to a flawed level so that your own flaws won't be so glaring, you're deceiving yourself.

We are all flawed; that is the reality of mortality. Don't tear others down. Lift them up, and you will find yourself lifted up as well.

CHAPTER TWENTY ONE

Learn to appreciate the smaller things in life; embrace things that make you feel stronger and wiser. I've learned that it is so much better to live without bitterness and resentment towards anyone. What others choose to say or do really has nothing to do with you. They act out their own frustrations, and sometimes you are in the line of fire.

Refusing to take the behavior of others personally is letting go and setting yourself free. The only thing that matters is what YOU think and feel and what response, if any, will give you the most peace.

For me, that's moving into a slower life. Quite rightly, it's time for the Taylor Swifts to have their day; I've had mine. It was heartening to see that at the grand old age of 82, our old friend Paul McCartney is still supporting the stars of the day like her.

When America's latest global megastar was performing at Wembley during her Eras tour, Paul was spotted dancing and singing with the crowd. As well as endorsing Taylor's talent, he wasn't too old or too grand to sing and dance with her fans in the crowd. What a mark of a humble man.

I hope that's the sort of man that I still am, and of course that I can still be up singing and dancing with people when I am Paul's age. I guess I'll have to see what the next decade has in store for me.

But this time, I'm really stepping down with the full intention of going fishing and getting to know all 15 of my grandchildren so much better—Cassidi, Clanci, Emma, Eve, Aspen, Andelyn, McCall, Easton, Keaton, Cruze, Lincoln, Ledger, Emmitt, Alexis, and Parker.

Over the years, fishing at my mother-in-law Velda's home in the Wasatch Mountains was a real sanctuary for me. It's where I have been able to relax and escape all the chaos that showbusiness brings with it. I've spent many happy hours there with my sons, and I hope to spend many more there in the company of my grandchildren.

Maybe I will even start reading, seeing that learning with books was never my focus growing up. I've always loved archaeology.

By now, you will have gleaned that my natural personality and my problems with perfectionism were not a good mix for any kind of robust mental health. When it was at its worst, it came at a price to my loved ones.

Mary doesn't want to lose me, so I am making a lot of adjustments. Boy, I've got a lot of catching up to do, especially living with a wife who was an English teacher and can so easily get through ten whole books a month!

Though I guess I will always be a seventies boy who loves rock 'n' roll, my performing days really have come to an end now. Unless, of course, there's a good cause somewhere that I can help by occasionally getting me back up there on stage...

While compiling this memoir, I've tried very hard to give you an honest account of my life as a member of the Osmond family. My hope is that you've come away with an accurate idea of who our parents, George and Olive, really were—their faith, personalities, values and ambitions as well as those of their children.

I do recognize that on some issues, nothing's better than hearing views that are direct from our parents at that time, which is why I've decided to include some articles written by George and Olive from our original fan magazine Osmonds' World from 1973 -1975 - Wise and Wonderful words.

MOTHER & FATHER

The following pages include words from my mother and father, written in the 1970s.

BY OLIVE OSMOND

George and I married in the Mormon Temple in Salt Lake City in December 1944 and on October 19th 1945, I became a mother. Our little George Virl Osmond Jr came to bless our home. I didn't know before then it was possible to love someone so much. I was extremely nervous with our first baby and I knew George was even more afraid, he had never been around babies! George enjoyed the children once they passed the tiny, delicate stage, I've often said how wise our Heavenly Father was in giving us eight boys and one girl!

When George and I had had our first eight children, we bought some land at Huntsville and that summer, began building our dream home. We hardly missed a day practicing our music and more and more requests were coming in for the boys to sing.

The Winter was busy, and so was the next Spring. Val Hicks continued working with the Boys to improve their harmony and had arranged for us to go back to Kansas City to perform for the International Barbershop Convention. It was their first train ride and the Evans Quartet from Salt Lake City went with them, they sang songs all along the way. The boys were still too young to belong to the Barbershop Organization, but they performed as guests and won lots of hearts. From then on, they were being asked to sing all over the country.

One of those singing engagements was at San Jose, California. It was to be their first plane ride and some of us were a little nervous about it! However, the Evans Quartet were along with us and that certainly helped. The Evans Quartet were on The Lawrence Welk Show and they got introduced to the Lennon Family.

We got an appointment to audition to Lawrence Welk but were told to be sure to call before coming. Bad news! Mr Welk couldn't make it, the audition was canceled and we were broken-hearted about the whole business. We decided to let the boys have a little bit of fun at least before we went home to Utah, so we took them to Disneyland. They always dressed alike when they were small and there they stood 'in uniform' watching and listening to a quartet dressed like policemen.

The boys were fascinated because they sang that same type of music, barbershop harmony!

By January 1963 we were living in Canoga Park, California, in one of Andy Williams' houses. We had a huge yard where the kids enjoyed playing ball, riding bikes and tricycles and doing various other activities. Alan, Wayne, Merrill and Jay were very busy about this time. They made quite a few appearances on The Andy Williams Show and they also had some singing and acting parts in the movie called "The Travels of Jaimie McPheeters." I guess it was really a TV series.

Donny was involved in the TV shows but not the movie, so I had Virl, Tom, Donny and Marie home with me. All the kids but Donny and Marie were enrolled in public school at the time and what a struggle that was. Because of their ages they were going to several different schools which meant that every time they had a call for the movie or TV show we would have to get special permission from the teachers and principal and special assignments to take to the studio school. (They were required to have three hours' schooling each day with the teacher from the Los Angeles School Board whenever they were working, and if they were traveling they had to take a teacher and welfare worker with them. California laws were very strict about this.) It was really quite a chore just to get them to work and school. George was by their side constantly.

Virl had enrolled at Canoga Park High School and Tom took special classes for the deaf at Mulholland Junior High. Because of their hearing problems both were a little shy and sometimes longed to be back home with their friends and in familiar surroundings. The move to California was a big adjustment for all of us in many ways. By the time we'd paid our booking agency, personal manager, union dues, travel expenses, costume expenses, choreographers, music arrangers and so forth we didn't have much left to live on.

When we had moved to California I was expecting again and spent most of my time at home with Virl, Tom and Marie. Once we had a special Valentine party and invited Andy (the boys were under a five-year contract appearing on The Andy Williams Show). There just aren't enough hours in the day, nor days in the week to do all the things we should like or would like to do.

We try hard not to offend anyone. We try never to refuse an autograph unless there's a safety problem of some kind in which someone might get hurt. There are very few hours we can have to ourselves or immediate family. Something is always "urgent and pressing."

Back to the Valentine Party. Quite a bit of fan mail had been coming in which was exciting. (I still have all those first letters in a scrapbook.) Just before the Valentine Party, a letter came addressed to Andy in care of us at our home address. It was from Ogden, Utah, our hometown so we thought it must be a special one - perhaps thanking Andy for giving us a "break" or something like that. We put it up on the fireplace where it would be safe and we could be sure to give it to the Williams family at the party. Jay Williams opened it and read it to all of us and we could have crawled under the table: Some lady was reprimanding Andy for "ruining one of the classics" (he and Martha Raye had done a comedy sketch about Goldilocks and the Three Bears).

Everyone thought it was hilarious—but the lady from Ogden thought they shouldn't have treated a classic that way. Father Williams assured us it was all right and told us to think nothing about it. He said there would be lots worse things than that to cope with and how right he was! He has given us lots of counsel and advice through the years, which has been most helpful. He's a wise man.

George had his real estate broker's license—so did Jay Williams, so they often used to travel together looking at property for investments. One day they were traveling around the San Fernando Valley and came across a Spanish-styled house where a couple of French ladies lived—a mother and daughter. The daughter was an artist and she had turned the house into an art gallery. It had a huge yard all fenced in and was very private.

Jay said, 'George, this would be an ideal place for your family. Why don't you consider it? If you don't want it, I'll buy it for Andy.'

George said: "Let's flip a coin to see who buys it." George won. Then he wondered if he had done the right thing. He came home and told us to start packing—that we were going to move.

When he took us to see it, he drove on some "angled" streets and I got my directions all mixed up. As a result, for me, for the eight years that we lived there the sun always came up in the South.

We moved to this house in the San Fernando Valley in March of 1963. Lots of work had to be done there, too. We cleaned, painted and remodeled just as we had done with every place we had ever lived in. We made a lovely home out of it. We had a big music room at the back which was especially nice for the Boys to practice their music and dancing.

We hired the choreographer from The Andy Williams Show, Jack Regas, and he used to really make them work learning new routines. He was a great guy and we'll always be grateful to him, too, for the help and encouragement he gave us. The routines they learned from him sort of changed their whole direction. After that they learned to play guitars as well as other instruments, and they began to forge ahead and gain the attention of young people.

One of the very important things we learned really early on in our career is that our lives have to be planned out almost like a military exercise—not only precisely but also well in advance. If we didn't do this we would never be able to manage a quarter of the things we actually do.

If George and I hadn't had a savings account to back us up, I'm sure we would have had to cut short the showbusiness career in those lean years. But we felt there was a reason we were doing these things. We knew the Boys were talented and as long as we were "getting by" we felt we should give them every single opportunity to carry on.

We learned that we had to put forth a lot of effort on our own. Unless we came up with something and different all the time, the Boys weren't used in Andy's show. No one seemed to really care or take time to give us suggestions or create anything special for the Boys to do. So, we tried to be creative ourselves. We'd search for good barbershop songs and then practice, practice, practice until they had the harmony down perfectly. George did what choreography he could—the "moves" as we called them. They learned precision (they would make the same gestures at the same time) and that became one of their "trademarks."

Jay Williams, Andy's father, was our champion—our hero. He always believed in the Boys and was delighted when they performed. They reminded him of his own boys, the Williams brothers when they first started. When we'd get a new routine learned, we would go to his house and perform for him and his wife, Florence. (The Kids loved them and called them Grandma and Grandpa Williams.) If he liked what he saw and heard, we could just bet that he'd recommend it to Andy, and the Boys would be back on the show the following week. It was one of these occasions that Donny sang "You Are My Sunshine" for him and he really was excited about it. Donny had imitated Andy (he had learned the song from one of Andy's records—a difficult arrangement—and he had every little detail right).

Andy wore V-necked sweaters in those days so he bought a little one for Donny just like his and they sang together. This was Donny's first appearance, The viewing audience began to respond with letters just like they did when the Quartet sang on the steps—so Andy usually included him in a solo spot somewhere.

I didn't go to the TV tapings nor watch the movie being filmed. I was "expecting" again, and no-one ever saw me in public very much then except perhaps at the grocery store occasionally. I stayed home with Virl, Tom and Marie and watched them on television. What a thrill!

The house we moved into in Canoga Park was a big, old, two-story frame. Jay Williams had just purchased it as part of Andy's investment program and it was quite run down. They offered to carpet it, paint it etc. before we moved in, but we were so eager to get a place to stay, we told them not to worry about it—we'd get it all cleaned up ourselves.

We scrubbed, painted and polished. We discovered a beautiful hardwood floor underneath an old, worn-out carpet so we pulled it up, refinished the floor and polished it "till it shone like a mirror." We had brought our new beautiful swag drapes from our home in Ogden so we hung them (they just fitted) and by February we had the house looking great.

We decided to have a party and invite all the Williams family and let them know how much we appreciated the opportunity they had given us. We prepared for days, decorated the living room with red and white streamers, etc. and had heart shaped cakes and home-made ice cream. Jay and Florence, Don and Marilyn and their twins, Andy and David, Bob and Edna and their family and Bob and Jane Daniels and their family came and had a good time. The Boys entertained (they had worked up a new number featuring Donny called I'm A Ding-Donged Daddy from Dumas). Andy and Claudine couldn't make it. They never did come to our house though they were invited several times. For a while we were a little "hurt" but gradually as we got caught up in the routines of showbusiness ourselves, we realized what a demanding thing it can really be.

We were always concerned about the laws of health. We wanted everyone to stay well. We were so busy we didn't have time to be ill, anyway!

Each morning George would grind enough wheat for our cereal and then about twice a week he would grind an extra amount very fine so I could make bread. We also had a cow and had plenty of milk, cream and butter. We bought a pasteurizer from Sears and would pasteurize about two gallons of milk each day. I'd skim the cream from the top and would make ice cream for Family night each week and churn butter with the excess. We canned a lot of fruit and put food away each fall to last us through the winter. We had planted a garden with fruit trees, berry plants and grape vines. The orchard produced fruit in abundance!

We decided to remodel our kitchen one day and put some new cabinets in. I thought maybe we'd get them for one side of the wall but when George ordered them, he had them put on three sides of the kitchen—including a built-in stainless steel stove top, double ovens, dishwasher, blender unit with attachments and the biggest stainless refrigerator I'd ever seen in a home. We were all delighted, but I felt George had been a little extravagant. One of his many ways of letting us know how much he loved us.

A little later he bought a few more cabinets, installed them himself on the fourth wall for a storage space for canned goods. We enjoyed that "pantry" so much and kept it stocked with good things for those special snack times. We always had a nice glass of fruit juice for breakfast each morning.

We had a griddle built into the stove top and one morning Virl decided to be a chef. He made a big paper hat, stretched a string and put clothes pins on it to take orders like they sometimes do in a short order house. He mixed up the pancake batter, set the table and then started yelling "Hotcakes for sale—one penny." We still remind him of that to this day.

Donny and Marie were just tiny about this time and used to be busy getting into things all the time. One day while I was washing clothes they were unusually quiet so I decided to check on them. I found them in my bedroom with their hands in a big jar of peanut butter. Marie looked up at me and her eyelashes were so heavy with peanut butter she could hardly open them. Donny looked so sheepish about the whole thing he just stared at me.

I dashed in the other room and grabbed the movie camera because I just knew they'd never believe me when they got older if I didn't have some proof. They had spread peanut butter on the walls and on the bedspread and all over themselves. What a pair. What one couldn't think of the other could. They've always been real pals—a little mischievous but always having fun.

There was just never a minute wasted from morning till night. We were so busy: I was the bookkeeper for our real estate and insurance business and I'd sit up late at night after everyone had gone to bed to work on the books.

I converted one little room into an office complete with desk, files, typewriter, adding machine and telephone. Then I could just close the door and keep everything safe and intact. We lived quite close to our main office, too, so George could call me, dictate a letter and then dash in and pick it up later.

We've always worked closely together and I believe that's one of the secrets of our happy marriage and happy family. "All for one and one for all" has always been one of our family mottos.

Tom was going to the Utah School for the Deaf at this time and one of our dear friends, Joe Deamer, would go out of his way each morning to pick him up and take him into town for us as he was going to work. He would never let us pay him anything—not even put gas in his car. He would just say, "What are you trying to do—deprive me of a blessing?" What a great man. I hope he knows how much we appreciate the kindness he showed to our little Tom.

Virl went to the Deaf School for one year but the teachers thought he had enough hearing to get by in public school with a hearing aid so we entered him into Junior High. He came home one day with his finger broken—he had been involved in a fight with some kid that made fun of him because he was wearing a hearing aid. He had to have a wire put through the bone and had quite a time getting it to heal but I think he was always a little proud of that broken finger to think he had enough spunk to face a bully.

Virl, Tom and Alan decided to take a summer class in woodworking. Alan was working with some electrical tool—a drill or an electric saw. Anyway, a piece of board broke off and cut his chin. Some of the fans have asked him how he got the scar. He was making a wooden horse plaque for me. Each of them made one. Virl also made a little lamp in the shape of a pump. The handle of the pump would turn the light on and off. I've always treasured those little things.

SOME OF MOTHER'S MEMORIES

The day Marie tried on an old dress of mine that was one of my favorites. (I guess that's why I had hung on to it all that time though it didn't fit me anymore!) It was pale pink. When Marie got to be about 14, she dug this dress out of the closet and came in to me wearing it—it fitted her perfectly. My! That took me back to my younger days and almost brought tears to my eyes to think that my own daughter was a real teenager and looked so pretty in my dress!

The first time Jimmy cooked me a meal—eggs on toast! He was so proud!

The day I first set eyes on George and thought that he was positively the most handsome man I had ever seen! He was the first man who made my heart beat faster.

When the boys first appeared on television a Walt Disney special filmed in California. I was so proud yet so nervous for them—I couldn't have been more nervous if I had had to go on TV myself!

The day we stopped calling Jim 'Little' Jimmy.

The times when George and I were young parents and we would take our children to the drive-in movies in their pajamas and they would fall asleep in the back of our station wagon.

The Christmas in Japan when some very kind people who were fans but really didn't know us at all, had a tiny Christmas tree delivered from a florist shop so that we wouldn't feel homesick.

How proud I was of a Christening dress I embroidered which I was determined to keep right through our family and then pass on to my grandchildren. I left spaces for seven of my own children's initials on the gown and would have hardly believed it if you had told me I would have nine children!

When we decided to start up our own magazine I was so excited I stayed awake almost all night planning out what we would put into it. I got the same kind of excitement from knowing that the Osmond story was going to be made into a book by our good friend Paul Dunn.

Traveling through Las Vegas many years ago and hearing Alan say that one day we would see the Osmonds' name up in lights. In 1971 his wish came true when my sons starred at Caesar's Palace. Before that they made second or share billing, too.

The very first time the family took to ice skates, which was long ago before the Donny and Marie Show was even thought of! On an Andy Williams show it was an idea somebody came up with and the children had to learn to skate quite well in no more than a few days!

Our first Family Nights when there were seven of us and we always brought out the best dinner service although at first I didn't have a complete set of dinner plates. Never mind, by candlelight everything looked that much grander!

The first time I rode on a powered cycle—I was scared!

Our first grandchild, Aaron, and how sweet he was. Luckily all our grandchildren are so cute and give us endless pleasure. Mind you, they have good parents! Aaron is still cute though he's a big boy now—nearly seven.

– Mother (Olive Osmond)

SOME OF FATHER'S MEMORIES

※

Riding round London town and the countryside nearby on my bicycle whilst I was stationed in Britain in the forties.

Meeting the Queen of England in 1972 and how sweet and regal she was. It was an awesome moment for all of us Osmonds and it was our first trip as a family.

The first time Jay wore a complete proper football kit and he looked a real sportsman. He was always very good at football and is still an athletic person.

The old cars Olive and I used to have when we were first married. Money was a bit tight to say the least and I always had to buy old used cars. One, a Chevrolet, had what you could call an open plan underneath, so you had to be careful your feet didn't go through the floor.

When we were first married and Olive in some ways had a lot more confidence than I did and she virtually pushed me into one of my jobs as a salesman. I soon found out that Olive was a wonderful partner in love and in business. I don't know which she excelled at most—raising a family or making a success of business ventures. Well—maybe raising a family, but she was wonderfully talented at so many different things.

How amazed I was the day Olive brought some old photos to me when we first met, and the photos turned out to be of me as a tiny baby. By the strangest coincidence Olive's mother had lodged with my mother many years before and held me often!

The time in California I won the toss and ended up buying a house which I didn't think was very beautiful at all! Still, the children enjoyed it and we managed to sell it again when the time came around!

Appearing on an Osmond TV special and singing with my boys. That was a moment to remember.

Seeing Marie on stage when she was only 13 years old and yet she was as mature in her act as many an adult performer. My little girl grown up!

Helping the boys to develop their singing skills and barbershop routines when they first started out. Right from the start The Osmonds were a real family act … We were right with the boys all the way and still are.

Donny when he first became popular as a solo artist and wore his now famous Donny caps. We would have to steam them to get all the creases out because pretty soon Donny was giving away a couple of dozen a performance, so we got them packed in big boxes—squashed down tight.

Purchasing my very own ranch—a dream I had always had. I love the outdoor life and so do all the children.

Being frightened to pick up Virl when he was a little baby, he seemed so tiny I feared I would hurt him! Now I couldn't pick him up if I tried!

SOME OF FATHER'S MEMORIES

The early days of our marriage when—although we were non-stop busy to get our various houses in order—we had a wonderful time. We learned that to live a happy life you must keep striving and must make the best of everything.

Meeting Mary, Suzanne and Kathlyn and realizing that I would have some wonderful new daughters around!

When the boys embark upon a tour or a series of cabaret dates you probably think to yourself, "Well that's nice, the Osmonds are coming round again." But I don't suppose it occurs to you—and why should it? —that this tour or this engagement was planned months ago; maybe even as long as a year.

This longsightedness may sound a bit silly to you but in fact it's a necessity. It does have its disadvantages—after all, if we plan a world tour for May 1975 and then decide in April 1975 that we really need a good long rest, well that's our hard luck! It would be far too late to back down, however badly we needed a holiday. But the benefits far outweigh the disadvantages. Let's look at it the other way, if we wait till April 1975 and then decide at the last minute that we want to do a big tour in May, we'd be disappointed. We would find that all the concert halls are booked solid. We'd find all our favorite support acts already with a full diary. And so on. In other words, in showbusiness you must be professional for your own benefit and for the benefit of those who work with you. And being professional means planning. Tours really are the most important things to get organized. They involve so many people and places that they really do take months to plan. We get together with manager Ed and work out the tour details. Most summers up till now we've done a two-month tour of America. So as soon as one is finished, we have a meeting to decide—will there be another one next year? If the answer is "yes" we must work out which cities we want to visit and then our staff start to phone up the concert halls, stadiums and so on in those cities to make a provisional booking to hire the place. After all, you can't have a tour without venues, so this is most important. If you ask early, you stand a good chance of getting the venue you want. Of course, our staff have to work out how long it will take us to get from one place to another without suffering from exhaustion. They wouldn't, for instance, book us in Toronto one night and Los Angeles the next because they are over three thousand miles apart!

Gradually the pattern of the tour builds up and soon we see how long it will take. Then we find a supporting act and backing musicians—we know we must do this early too or else we might have to make do with second best.

Now with one or two tours like this slotted into our year, we already have a skeleton plan to work on. We also know one or two other things we can pencil in. For instance, we know that if at all possible, we want to be at home for Christmas. We also know that we need two or three months of the year for writing and recording material for the boys' and Marie's singles and albums.

Obviously, we can't plan every little thing months in advance—for instance, some of the boys' TV appearances aren't arranged until a week or two before they happen. What we have to do is to try to get our priorities right.

Let me give you an example. For some time now, a trip to Russia has been on the cards. That is something all the family very much wants to do. It is something we have looked forward to for a long time but haven't been able to organize as far as dates and places go because we hadn't the official go-ahead. However, we knew that it was almost certain it would happen sometime in 1974. All we could do in that case was to keep our plans as fluid as possible and then when the Russian dates were confirmed, we could, if anything clashed, do a bit of juggling with our year's schedule.

SOME OF FATHER'S MEMORIES

The next thing Mother, the boys and I like to get organized as early as we can is the album releases. Once we know the likely completion date of an album we can do a lot around that—for example, when the boys make TV appearances they usually tie in with the release of a record. So, the same applies to singles. If we know we've an Osmond single coming out, we can let people know early so that if, perhaps, someone wants to invite the Osmonds onto a TV show, they will know when is the best time and we can be hopeful of getting maximum coverage for any one record. It would be bad planning, I'd say, to have the Osmonds doing three top-line TV shows when their current single is going down the charts and they aren't going to release a new one for another six weeks. The sensible time for everyone concerned for the boys to do TV shows would be during the weeks prior to and just after the release of a new disc.

So, by this time our diary is beginning to look quite full. What gaps there are, without a doubt, will all be filled by the time those dates arrive. We might get invited to a special dinner or to make a special personal appearance. A really fun TV show might come along, or a network might want to do a talk program with us.

An exciting new development is that all our records in future in America are going to be released on the Kolob label—that is, our own records.

Jimmy is working on an album—and would you believe it, the family have persuaded ME to venture into the recording scene! Yes, me! They say I have a nice voice and so I'm starting to work which may or may not get to see the light of day! Really it is for our own private enjoyment, but if it turns out okay you may get to hear yet more of the Osmond family on record. (I bet you thought we had come to the end of the line with Jimmy and Marie, didn't you?)

Or, at long last, a movie script might turn up. We've been waiting for the right movie for so long now. Every month we hope it will turn up. And when it does we're going to want to go to work as soon as possible. Maybe then we'll have to do some of that "shuffling round" I was telling you about earlier!

Then there are always interviews and photo-sessions to be done—luckily, they can mostly be planned only a week or so early to fit in with other work dates.

And lastly, if there's any time left at all during our busy year, we might even take a holiday. But you can bet that when it comes to forward planning, our vacation has to take a back seat. There's always somewhere we can go to soak up the sun and relax, even at only a day's notice!

Stop Press: Literally as I write this, word has come through that it is virtually definite that the boys will start work on a film in September, isn't it exciting? I can tell you without hesitation that my boys will all be very, very pleased and I'm sure they can't wait to get started. This is the big moment that we have been anticipating for a couple of years—a new venture for the boys to work out.

– Father (George Osmond)

Here Father talks in 1976 about his position and the things he has taught the children.

As the head of the household, I "officially" have the last word about how the family should be run, major decisions and so on but as you can imagine with Olive as my wife and with such fine children, I rarely have any occasion to use authority. I believe that the best decisions are those made jointly by the whole family and as we usually think along the same lines this is what mostly happens.

I've always known that the best way to run a home is on love and understanding and I would rather have things as they should be by being persuasive rather than by using force! I remember when Virl was born wondering if a difficult task would be knowing how and when to discipline Virl and any other children Olive and I would be fortunate enough to have. Should I be lenient and kind? Strict and strong? I wanted to strike a good middle road, and I prayed to God that I would be a fair and good father.

I need not have worried. With guidance from the Church and help from Olive things worked out very well. I was very strict with the children—and can still be if the need arises—but I have always let them know how much I love them. If I have to scold them and put them right, they know I am doing it because I love them and because I want them to be happy.

For instance, if you don't learn about things like telling the truth, being unselfish, compassion, patience and respect, you can't get the best out of life and you can't give the best. So, I enjoyed teaching the children these things as they grew up. I tried to teach by example and by reading from The Bible and The Book of Mormon, and if ever they went wrong, I would not merely tell them off but show them the right way. I would try to replace a negative deed with a positive thought.

I think that if a child needs to be scolded, he also deserves to be told why he has been scolded and what he should have done instead. This way you build on the good things while taking away the bad.

Olive always says to me that she spoils the children and then I must undo what she has done! She's partly right—she is a warm-hearted mother and soft with her children.

I've always had a wonderful relationship with Marie. She was born on my birthday, so I tell everyone else that she's mine so keep away! Mind you, I tell her off too because like any teenage daughter she can be a bit of a handful sometimes!

I kid Marie that I won't let her date until she is 18 instead of 16, and the boys do too! They are going to be very fussy about who they let her go out with! She just laughs and reminds us that it is only a little over a year to go before she can date, and that's a time she is looking forward to!

Seriously, I feel that it is important to give sons and daughters the feeling that the family is all working together—that it is necessary to all play a part in family life and each has his special role to play.

I believe that you should try to treat children as much like adults as possible. They love it. If you treat them like adults they usually respond like adults. I felt that all my children were important as people and needed to feel important and I think I have been right.

The boys and Marie have been a credit to Olive and me. And what is so wonderful is that I can look at our little grandchildren with Tommy and Virl and see the same wonderful relationship blossoming in a new generation—and to me that is all I need to make me feel I did things 'my way' but right!

– FATHER

TRIBUTES

THE BAND

Ralph Walsh – Sound/Front of House Engineer:
It's difficult to sum up in a few words how the time I have spent with Merrill, his family and band has influenced me, progressed me, given me confidence and a terrific working and social environment.

It took time; our early days spent working on the show meant looking at how we could constantly better things, be able to provide the best we could to the audiences who supported Merrill over the years. When we got there, with team effort from Merrill, myself and the band, we had something special. It showed as audiences got bigger, our reputation grew and the show was at its best. What a way to finish.

Socially, our times together were some of the best I will ever remember: the back stage laughs, stories and jokes. Merrill walking on stage with tears of laughter in his eyes and myself giggling as I walk toward the mixing desk to start a show—these made things extra special, and proved such friendships between all of us.

I am eternally grateful, humbled and honored for the opportunity to work with the lead singer from one of the biggest family names in musical history – The Osmonds.

I wish Merrill, Mary & the entire family the very best for the future, and look forward to phone calls, messages & emails as we keep in contact – the music will live on, and the laughs will continue!

Pat Windebank – Bass Player, Musical Director/Arranger:
As your bass player, Merrill, I've had the incredible privilege of standing beside a true legend.

Your voice—rich, soulful, and unmistakably powerful—has been the soundtrack for a generation. You've moved hearts, uplifted spirits, and brought joy to countless people through your music

The way you've carried yourself with such professionalism, kindness, and grace over the years only adds to the immense respect you've earned. With immense respect and gratitude, I am forever your friend.

David Wallace – Drummer:
It's starting to sink in, this will be Merrill's last concerts and I feel a little sad but, it's been a pleasure and an absolute honor to work with him, I could have never imagined (at four-five years old watching the Osmonds on TV) that I'd have the opportunity to work / play / spend time with any of them.

I will always treasure the fun I've had playing these tunes; the happy touring memories together; our many heart-felt conversations and millions of laughs we've shared over the years.

From the bottom of my heart, Merrill: Thank you, Sir, it's been an absolute blast!

Wishing You, Mary and all the family health, happiness and much love for the future. There's always a place to stay for you guys here.

Phil Hendriks – Vocals and Guitar:
I was ten years old when The Osmonds arrived in the UK as an unstoppable force in 1972. Over the next year or two, they seemed to be the biggest act on the planet.

Every girl in my class at school would be carrying around some piece of Osmond or Donny memorabilia. My sister bought the 'Crazy Horses' album and 'The Plan' and played them incessantly. Whilst it may not have been 'cool' for young guys to admit to liking them, I had to confess that those records became part of my musical consciousness and I grew to love them, particularly the exciting, rockier numbers like 'Goin' Home', 'Crazy Horses' etc.

The ten-year-old me could never have imagined that one day I would share the stage with the lead singer so, in November 2020, it was to my great honor that I was asked to step in as Merrill's guitarist for a live internet concert broadcast from London.

Since then, I've played on all of Merrill's live shows. Merrill is not just a consummate professional but he's also one of the nicest guys in showbusiness. A warm, friendly man with a great sense of humor and an absolute pleasure to work with. Thanks for the experience, Merrill, I've loved every minute!

TRIBUTES TO MY CHILDREN

TRAVIS MERRILL

My eldest son, Travis, has not only been a leader in our family, but also a great example to his siblings. He is a loving and devoted father and a wonderful husband to his wife, Maggon. His strong faith in God and testimony of eternal families is a constant source of inspiration and guidance for our family. I am truly blessed to have had him as a son.

JUSTIN ALAN

Justin is not just a remarkable son, but a shining example of determination and resilience. Despite facing numerous obstacles throughout his life, he has consistently shown that he is capable of overcoming them with unwavering faith in God and the power of positivity. His relentless determination has allowed him to conquer mountains and achieve great success. I am proud to pay tribute to my son who serves as an inspiration to us all.

SHANE GEORGE

My son, Shane, has shown resilience, forgiveness and unwavering faith. He has always remained true to his values and beliefs despite the difficulties he has faced. His love for the Lord, his wife Brittney and his children are a constant source of inspiration for all who know him. I am so grateful to have him as my son. Shane will always be known as my antidote.

HEATHER

Heather is truly a blessing in my life and I am grateful for her every day. Heather has a heart of gold and always puts others before herself. Her talents, particularly her beautiful voice, bring joy to all those around her. I am so proud to call her my daughter and I know she will continue to spread love and positivity wherever she goes.

TROY DEAN

My dear son, Troy, who is our guardian angel, was sent to teach us the true meaning of unconditional love. Even after his passing, he continues to guide and teach us from the other side. Every day, we pray that we can live up to his perfect example of love and forgiveness towards others. He truly embodied the characteristics of Christ and serves as a reminder for us to strive for the same.

SHEILA

Sheila's journey has been full of challenges and heartache, but she has shown incredible strength and resilience. Despite the adversity she has faced she has not lost her faith in God and believes one day her joy will one day be fulfilled. She has shown remarkable determination to move forward and has not let her past define her.

Her story is a testament to the power of perseverance and serves as an inspiration to all those who face difficult times in their lives.

There's one individual I feel impressed to acknowledge, known only by the code of 'Bountiful'. This is a soul who watches quietly, interprets with clarity and then seeks divine guidance on how to best serve the poor. He does not seek recognition. He stays in the background. These rare souls will appear, often without notice, just when we need them the most.

    I love you, Bountiful

FOOTNOTE

To sum up, having been the lead singer on 27 gold and platinum records, over 100,000 record sales and nominated for two Grammy Awards, knighted by two amazing organizations, and having traveled the world while meeting with legends like Elvis Presley, Robert Redford, Michael Jackson, Tom Jones, Led Zeppelin, Garth Brooks, Neil Diamond, the Queen of England, and two U.S. Presidents, it has been a journey of marvel.

I am so blessed that fans still follow my work and my words via new platforms that did not exist—or were even dreamed of—when my career began.

Here, I would like to share some of the 'Friday Messages' that I have posted on my Facebook page and which continues to keep us connected:

My dear friends,
Rather than believing someone who says they love you, trust someone who demonstrates their love for you. Actions speak louder than words. If someone truly loves you, they will show it through their actions. It is important to look for signs of

unconditional love, such as being there when you need them, supporting you, and being patient and understanding.

You're loved, Merrill

My dear friends,
Don't be surprised when a miracle shows up when you least expect it. Someone very special is praying for you right now, and their prayers are powerful. Trust in the power of prayer and have faith that good things will come your way. Keep an open mind and heart, and be prepared for blessings beyond your wildest dreams.

You're loved, Merrill

My dear friends,
Taking a calculated risk can lead to new opportunities and growth, both personally and professionally. It allows us to step out of our comfort zones and challenge ourselves, leading to potential rewards and success. On the other hand, not taking any risks can lead to a stagnant and unfulfilling life, always wondering about the "what ifs" and never truly knowing our full potential. So don't be afraid to take a chance and see where it could lead you.

You're loved, Merrill

My dear friends,
When you finally understand the big picture, you will understand why you went through all those struggles and challenges. You'll see that it was all part of a greater plan, leading you to where you are meant to be. Trust in the process, have faith and the future will reveal itself in due time.

You're loved, Merrill

FOOTNOTE

My dear friends,
We should all strive to live a life of integrity and moral uprightness. We should always strive to do the right thing even when it's difficult. We should treat others with kindness, compassion, and respect, and stand up for what is just and fair. Pursuing righteousness will not only bring personal fulfillment, but also contribute to a more just and harmonious society.
You're loved, Merrill

My dear friends,
It's important to remember that we can't control others' actions, but we can control our own. This means taking responsibility for our own thoughts, emotions, and behaviors, and not trying to force or change others. By focusing on ourselves and our own actions, we can create a more positive and peaceful environment for ourselves and those around us.
You're loved, Merrill

Thank you for reading

As a thank you for reading my book, you can listen to some of my music—free of charge.

1. Point your smartphone camera at the image below
2. Click the link that appears

Having trouble? Go to:
merrillosmond.com/black-bear-songs

Printed in Dunstable, United Kingdom